HARMONY BOOK FOR BEGINNERS

A Text Book and Writing Book for the First Year's Work, for Class, Private and Self Instruction, including Scales, Intervals, Common Chords, the Dominant Seventh Chord and Melody Making

BY

PRESTON WARE OREM

THEODORE PRESSER CO.
1712 CHESTNUT STREET
•PHILADELPHIA•

Printed in U.S.A.
F

Copyright, 1916, by THEODORE PRESSER Co.
British Copyright Secured

FOREWORD

———o———

THERE are many Harmony Books, and there will be many more. The Art of Music is in process of continual development and its practical side must be approached from various angles. It is not the function of a Beginner's Book to speculate or to advance new theories, but rather to deal with things as they are.

This work aims to present in a plain and practical manner the groundwork of Harmony, giving sufficient material for the work of the First Year, and affording a thorough preparation for more advanced study according to any of the standard methods.

Acting upon the principle of doing one thing at a time and doing it thoroughly, this work proceeds by easy stages, devoting special attention to Scales and Intervals, and to the handling of Common Chords. The subject matter is presented in such a manner as to develop the reasoning faculty from the very outset. On this account the Harmonizing of Melodies is introduced as early as possible, and the Figured Bass is held back to the point when it will be of real use rather than a matter of mere mechanical imitation. Working Principles, based upon present approved usages, are given to cover the various processes. There are no Rules; hence, there can be no confusing exceptions to worry the beginner. There are no foot-notes or cross references. Everything needed is in the body of the text, in its proper place.

All the Examples and Exercises are made as pleasing as possible from the musical standpoint in order to develop taste and discrimination from the beginning. Suggestions for Ear Training are given throughout. Ample space is provided for writing all of the Exercises directly in the book, thus giving the student a permanent record of the work done. Melody Making is introduced in order to stimulate the imagination and the creative faculty, thus encouraging the student to early efforts in original composition and laying a logical foundation for future study in this direction. Throughout the book continual stress is laid upon the analytical or inductive side.

HOW TO USE THIS BOOK

———o———

As the language of this book is chiefly colloquial, in the manner of a teacher addressing a class, it is suggested that each Chapter be read out aloud at the lesson, paragraph by paragraph, either by the teacher or by a student. In the case of Self Instruction reading aloud is no less necessary.

The thirty Chapters should answer for the usual forty weeks' work of the scholastic year, allowing for repetition and reviews and for an examination at the close of the year. No Chapter need be hurried through and none need be left until it is mastered.

Aim to train both the eye and the ear and to cultivate the imagination. Try everything and listen to it carefully. Write nothing without striving to imagine how it sounds. Verify this afterward by playing or singing it. Learn to know Scales, Intervals, and Chords by their looks, without having to spell them out, just as one knows a word at sight. Learn to analyze what is heard.

Let each paragraph as it is read be discussed freely and fully. Play both the examples and the exercises many times over. Never be contented with an exercise which does not sound satisfactory. Never pass by anything which is not thoroughly understood and mastered.

Write all the exercises in the spaces provided in the book, using a *medium soft lead pencil* for the purpose. Before writing in the exercises, however, work them out on a separate slip of paper or music writing tablet. Put them in the book only after they have been worked out satisfactorily.

Pay strict attention to the Questions at the ends of Chapters. Always be able to answer these correctly and in your own language, at all times.

CONTENTS

		PAGE
Foreword		iii
How to Use This Book		iv

CHAPTER

I.	Preliminary	7
II.	Further Preliminary Work	8
III.	The Scale	9
IV.	The Major Scale Continued	12
V.	Intervals	16
VI.	Intervals Continued	19
VII.	Further Consideration of Intervals	22
VIII.	Triads	27
IX.	Common Chords	31
X.	Common Chords in Succession	35
XI.	Harmonizing a Melody	39
XII.	Harmonizing a Melody Continued	44
XIII.	The First Inversion	47
XIV.	Harmonizing Melodies Resumed	53
XV.	Degree Names—The Second Inversion	55
XVI.	Second Inversion Continued	58
XVII.	Cadences	63
XVIII.	Harmonizing Melodies Resumed	68
XIX.	The Minor Scale	72
XX.	Harmony in the Minor	78
XXI.	Harmony in the Minor Continued	89
XXII.	The Figured Bass	94
XXIII.	The Figured Bass Continued	98
XXIV.	Melodies and Figures	103
XXV.	Freer Use of Chords and Inversions	106
XXVI.	Additional Uses of the Second Inversion	113
XXVII.	The Dominant Seventh Chord	121
XXVIII.	Inversions of the Dominant Seventh Chord	127
XXIX.	Further Uses of the Dominant Seventh Chord—Sequences	134
XXX.	On Melody Making	140

HARMONY BOOK FOR BEGINNERS

CHAPTER I
PRELIMINARY

There are certain terms and definitions which should be learned and understood thoroughly before proceeding further into the subject of Harmony.

The student may already be familiar with some or all of the following, but even in this case it is well to recapitulate.

To begin with, **Sound** is the result of *sound-waves* or vibrations of the air.

From the scientific standpoint, that branch of Physics which treats of the investigation of sound phenomena is known as **Acoustics**. With this study the practical musician has little to do, although it has many fascinations for the theorist.

Musical Sound is produced by regular or continuous vibration; **Noise**, by irregular vibration. As a class in Harmony cannot too soon begin to practice ear-training, it is suggested that practical illustrations of the foregoing definitions be had at once. Let the Pianoforte and other instruments be tried for examples of musical sounds and vibrations and let various hard objects be struck or dropped upon the floor or table in order to produce noises of various kinds.

The term **Tone** is applied to any musical sound.

Harmony is the combination of **Tones**.

In the making of music **twelve tones are employed**. For purposes of illustration let us refer to the keyboard of the Pianoforte. Starting from *Middle C* the white keys C, D, E, F, G, A, B give us seven tones and the black keys between C and D, D and E, F and G, G and A, A and B give us the remaining five tones. These twelve tones repeat themselves in varying depth or intensity, or in various **Octaves**, as they are called.

As an ear-training exercise, strike slowly and consecutively the seven white keys, beginning at middle C. Then, in the same manner, strike all twelve keys, both white and black. Afterwards, repeat the same processes, beginning with every other C upon the keyboard. This and some of the other preliminary exercises may seem very simple to the student, but it is only by slow and progressive stages, beginning with the utmost simplicity and never neglecting a step at any stage, that a good, practical working knowledge of harmony is to be obtained.

QUESTIONS

1. What is Sound?
2. What is Acoustics?
3. What is Musical Sound?
4. What is Noise?
5. What is a Tone?
6. What is Harmony?
7. How many Tones are used to make Music?
8. What are they?
9. What is an Octave?

CHAPTER II

FURTHER PRELIMINARY WORK

In the preceding chapter we spoke of Tones and of the twelve Tones used in the making of Music. In playing these tones we find that they differ in certain respects: some are high, some are low. In explanation of this fact we employ the term **Pitch**. Pitch is the relative intensity of vibration, the acuteness or gravity, the highness or lowness, of a musical sound. The more numerous the vibrations in any given time, the higher the sound; the fewer the vibrations the deeper the sound.

An ear-training exercise in Pitch may be made very interesting. In addition to the Pianoforte, as many other instruments as possible should be introduced. All pitches from the lowest to highest should be sounded and an effort be made to detect the vibrations.

A **Half-Step**, or **Semi-Tone**, is the smallest difference in Pitch which can be found upon the Keyboard of the Pianoforte. It is the least difference in Pitch in general use.

A **Whole Step**, or **Whole Tone** is the equivalent of two Half-Steps.

On the Keyboard of the Pianoforte or Organ, from any Key to the next adjacent Key, white or black, is a Half-Step or Semi-Tone; from any Key to the next Key but one, white or black, is a Whole Step or Whole Tone. For instance, from C to D♭, E to F, F♯ to G are Half-Steps; From C to D, E to F♯, A♭ to B♭, B♭ to C are Whole Steps.

The foregoing proposition cannot be too well learned and understood. In this case both the mind and the ear are to be trained. The student should go no further until the difference between Half and Whole Steps be clear to the mind and readily appreciated by the ear. Think and listen.

Just another definition: A **Degree** is a step: The step may be either a Half-Step or a Whole Step, but it is always from one letter to the next letter. For instance, A to B is a Whole Step, B to C is a Half-Step; both are Degrees.

As a matter of mutual understanding, we will not, in this work, employ the term **Note**, when we mean **Tone**. One may sound a Tone but not a Note. A **Note** is a written or printed character used to indicate the Pitch and Duration of a Tone.

It is presupposed that the student is familiar with the elements of Musical Notation, before taking up the study of this book.

QUESTIONS

1. What is Pitch?
2. What is a Half-Step?
3. What is a Whole Step?
4. Give examples.
5. What is a Degree?
6. Give examples.
7. What is a Note?

CHAPTER III

THE SCALE

A **Scale** or **Tone-Ladder** is a series or succession of tones arranged in regular order, ascending or descending.

There are many forms of Scales in use, but we have to deal at present with that particular form known as the **Major Scale**.

The **Major Scale** consists of eight degrees, arranged as follows: from the 1st to the 2nd degree, and from the 2nd to the 3rd are Whole Steps; from the 3rd to the 4th degree is a Half-Step; from the 4th to the 5th degree, and from the 5th to the 6th, and from the 6th to the 7th are Whole Steps; from the 7th to the 8th degree is a Half-Step. Briefly, for purposes of memorizing, the formula is: the *Half-Steps* are from 3 to 4 and 7 to 8; all the others are *Whole Steps*.

Let us turn to the key-board of the Pianoforte. Starting from Middle C, let us build a Major Scale.

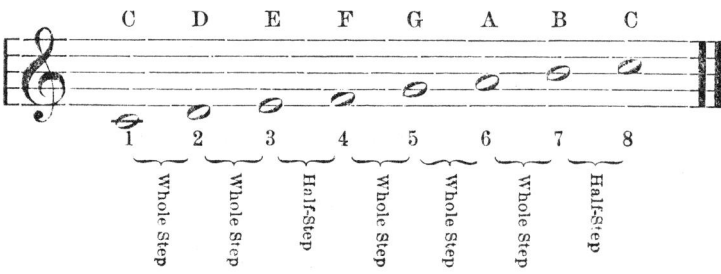

The eight white keys in their natural order, starting from Middle C, are found to produce a Major Scale, according to our formula. Play this scale many times and listen to it closely. The student *must always* be able to *recognize* the Major Scale upon hearing it played **or** sung.

We note that this particular major scale, which we have formed on the white keys, begins and ends on C. Hence we call it the Scale of **C Major**. To the degree or letter upon which any scale begins and ends we give the name **Tonic** or **Key Note**.

We further note that the Major Scale seems to consist of two equal portions. Let us examine:

To these series of four sounds each (arranged in this manner: Whole Step, Whole Step, Half-Step) we apply the term **Tetrachord**; and we find the Major Scale to consist of two Tetrachords separated by a Whole Step. Any Tone may become the Tonic of a Major Scale, or, putting it the other way about, **a Major Scale may be formed, beginning on any given Tone.**

Let us experiment a little, add another Tetrachord to the two we already have, and see what happens.

Leaving a Whole Step, we find that our additional Tetrachord is to begin on D. Proceeding from D, a Whole Step will give us E. So far, so good. We now want a Whole Step from E, whereas F (the next degree) is but a Half-Step. To correct this let us take the black key F♯. From E to F♯ is a Whole Step (two Half-Steps), and now we have the proper distance. Furthermore, from F♯ to G is a Half-Step, and our new Tetrachord is now complete.

An examination of the above discloses the fact that, in addition to a new Tetrachord, we have also formed a new scale.

Take the Tetrachord G, A, B, C, followed by the Tetrachord D, E, F♯, G, and we have the Scale of G.

Scale of G

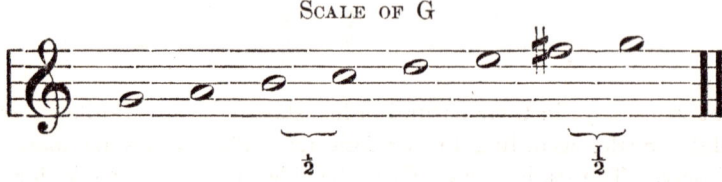

Now, let us start with the Tetrachord D, E, F♯, G, and follow on with still another Tetrachord, beginning on A. From A to B is a Whole Step, but from B to C is but a Half-Step. Correcting this, we change C to C♯, giving a Whole Step from B to C♯. Then, from C♯ to D is a Half-Step, as required.

We now have the Scale of D.

Before proceeding further, play all these Scales and Tetrachords, and let the ear verify all that has been done. Let the teacher or one of the students play incorrect Scales and Tetrachords in which the Whole and Half-Steps are improperly placed, and have the members of the class correct them.

As a writing exercise every student should first write out in musical notation Tetrachords beginning on C, G, D, A, E, B, F♯; then, write out in full Scales beginning on C, G, D, A, E, B.

THE SCALE

WRITING EXERCISE

Write Tetrachords, starting respectively from the notes given below.

WRITING EXERCISE

Write Scales in full.

In the preceding work in Scale construction it will have been noted that the Scales seem to overlap. That is to say, the second Tetrachord of one Scale becomes the first Tetrachord of the following Scale. From this fact we derive a principle: Scales having a *Tetrachord in common* are called **Related Scales.**

QUESTIONS.

1. What is a Scale?
2. Describe the Major Scale.
3. How are Major Scales named?
4. What is meant by the Tonic?
5. What is a Tetrachord?
6. How many Tetrachords in a Major Scale?
7. What is meant by the term Related Scales?

CHAPTER IV

THE MAJOR SCALE CONTINUED

In constructing the Major Scale be careful of two points:—Do not write two notes of the same degree in succession; for instance, A and A♯. Do not skip a letter; for instance, A♯ to C. Always write out the notes first, making an outline of the scale; then fill in the sharps, or flats, as needed. For instance, let us write the scale of F♯ Major.

To begin with, we make an outline, thus:

Now begin to add the needed sharps: F♯ (the Tonic or Key Note) to G♯ is a Whole Step, G♯ to A♯ is a Whole Step, A♯ to B is a Half-Step; and our first Tetrachord is complete. A Whole Step from B gives C♯; then C♯ to D♯ is a Whole Step, D♯ to E♯ is a Whole Step, E♯ to F♯ is a Half-Step; and our Scale is complete.

F♯ Major

At this point the student should write out for himself the Scale of C♯. It will be discovered that every note will need a Sharp.

Write out the Scale of C♯ Major.

Let us turn back for a little and attempt the construction of a Scale on F.

From F to G is a Whole Step, G to A, a Whole Step, but from A to B is also a Whole Step. Some way must be found for correcting this. Where notes would be a Half-Step too high without them we must introduce Flats; so we write B♭. Then, from A to B♭ is a Half-Step, and all is well, thus:

The remainder of the scale is easy: C, D, E, F.

F Major

At this point the student should write out, and play, the Scales of B♭ and E♭ Major.

THE MAJOR SCALE CONTINUED

Write out the Scales of B♭ and E♭ Major.

Returning to the Scale of F♯, previously constructed, let us take advantage of the fact that F♯ and G♭ are identical in Pitch, sounding exactly the same, and let us write out the Scale of G♭. This is known as an **Enharmonic Change**. An **Enharmonic Change** is a change of notation, or method of writing, without any change in sound.

Now for the Scale of G♭ Major: from G♭ to A♭ is a Whole Step, A♭ to B♭, Whole Step, B♭ to C♭, Half-Step; from D♭ to E♭ is a Whole Step, E♭ to F, Whole Step, F to G♭, Half-Step, thus:

G♭ MAJOR

Play this Scale, and, in point of sound, we find it to coincide with the Scale of F♯ Major.

Let the student write out, and play, the Scale of C♭ Major. Then right beside it let him write out the Scale of B Major. These will also be found to coincide in point of sound.

Write here the Scale of C♭ Major.   Write here the Scale of B Major.

Finally, let the student write out all the Major Scales in the following order: C, G, D, A, E, B and C♭ (Enharmonic), F♯ and G♭ (Enharmonic), C♯ and D♭ (Enharmonic), A♭, E♭, B♭, F. This is sometimes called the **Circle of Scales**. It will be observed an additional ♯ is needed in each scale as one advances, until seven ♯'s are employed, and that, going on from the Scale of C♭, one ♭ less is needed in each Scale.

All Major Scales as indicated.

Let the student now gather the sharps or flats used in constructing each Scale and place them in a group immediately after the Clef-sign, thus:

Each of these is known as the **Signature** of its respective Scale. In writing Signatures, it is customary, to place the sharps or flats in the order of their entrance into the Scales.

The Scales with their Signatures and the numbers and names of sharps or flats in each must now be memorized by the student.

THE MAJOR SCALE CONTINUED

QUESTIONS AND TESTS

1. What must be borne in mind in constructing Major Scales?
2. What is the best manner of procedure?
3. What is an Enharmonic Change?
4. Describe the Circle of Scales.
5. What is meant by the Signature?
6. How many sharps in C♯ Major? In A? In B? In F♯?
7. How many flats in C♭ Major? In F? In E♭? In A♭? In B♭?
8. Write out the Signatures of all Scales having flats, from one flat onward.
9. Write out the Signatures of all Scales having sharps, from one sharp onward.

Write out Signatures of

CHAPTER V
INTERVALS

An **Interval** is the measure of the *distance* or *difference* in *pitch* between any two musical sounds.

An Interval may be formed by any two tones, either sounded simultaneously, or in succession. If sounded simultaneously, a **Harmonic Interval** is constituted; if, in succession, it is known as a **Melodic Interval**.

For example, this is a Harmonic Interval:— 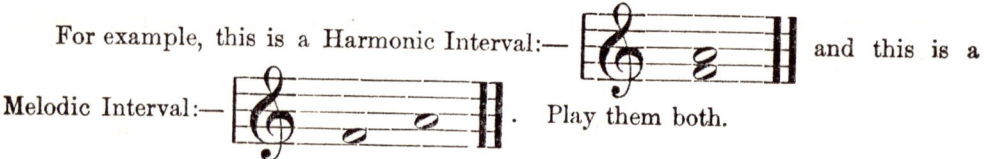 and this is a Melodic Interval:— . Play them both.

An Interval is **named** according to the *number of letters* included. Thus, the Interval from C to D is called a *Second*, (two letters being concerned); from C to E is a *Third*, (three letters being concerned: C, D, E); in a like manner, from C to F is a *Fourth*, from C to G is a *Fifth*, etc.

Always reckon Intervals from the *lower note upward*, and count the number of letters, including those upon the notes out of which the Interval is formed.

When two voices or instruments sound the same tone, there is no difference in pitch. This is called a **Unison** or **Prime**. Strictly speaking, it is not an Interval at all.

Let us write out the Intervals to be found in the Scale of C Major, reckoning from the Tonic upward.

Sing and play them all many times. Let the teacher or a student play them, and let the others endeavor to name them.

In a similar manner write out the Intervals in all the other Scales, using the proper Signatures. Then play and sing them and endeavor to name them as before.

INTERVALS IN ALL SCALES

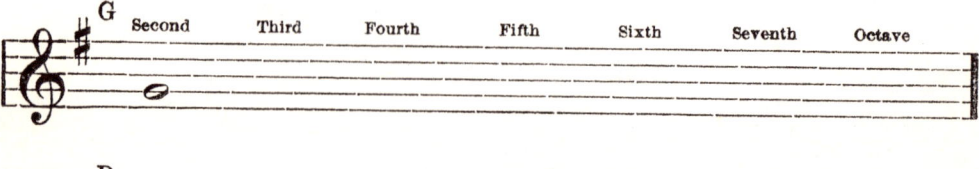

INTERVALS

This exercise is *imperative*. A working knowledge of the Intervals is the basis of all musical construction. They cannot be too well learned, and this is only the beginning of it.

OREM'S HARMONY BOOK

QUESTIONS AND TESTS

1. What is an Interval?
2. How does the Harmonic Interval differ from the Melodic Interval?
3. How is an Interval named?
4. How do you reckon Intervals?
5. What is a Unison?
6. What other name has it?
7. Name the following Intervals:

8. Write the following Intervals, using proper signatures:
   In the Scale of D: Fourth, Seventh, Second.
   In the Scale of B♭: Third, Fifth, Fourth.
   In the Scale of E: Second, Sixth, Third.

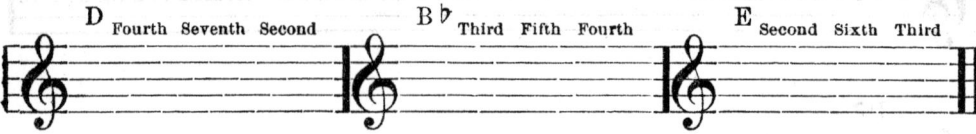

9. Write Octaves in the Scales of E♭, F♯, B:

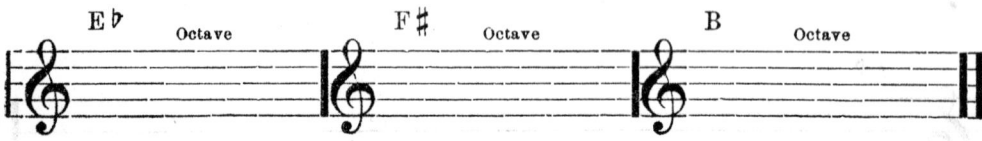

CHAPTER VI
INTERVALS CONTINUED

As an additional writing and ear-training exercise, let the student write and play all the Intervals in each scale which can be formed by employing any two degrees of each scale. For instance, take the second degree of the Scale of C, D, and write Seconds, Thirds, etc., above D; then take E and do likewise; and so on.

The foregoing exercise having been completed, let us plunge deeper into the subject of Intervals.

We now know, in a general way, how to name an Interval, but each named Interval may be one of several **kinds**, or specific varieties.

Let us illustrate: according to our method of arriving at the *Name of an Interval*, C to D is called a Second, but C to D♭ must also be called a Second, since only two letters are involved, in either case. Let us look at these Seconds, and play them:

Similarly try these Sixths:

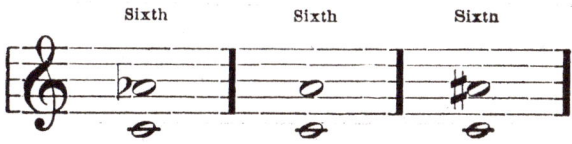

All are Sixths, but each has a different sound.

To return to our Seconds: C to D and C to D♭; let us count the Half-Steps in each. From C to D is a Whole Step or two Half-Steps, but from C to D♭ is a Half-Step. This experiment leads us to the general principle:

The **Kind** or **Variety** of an Interval depends upon the number of Half-Steps.

The **Major Scale** furnishes us with a **Standard of Measurement** for all Intervals. To any of the **Normal Intervals** of the Major Scale which can be formed from its **Tonic** to **Any Other Degree** we apply the terms **Major** or **Perfect**.

The **Seconds, Thirds, Sixths** and **Sevenths** thus produced are called **Major**. The **Fourths** and **Fifths** are called **Perfect**. An explanation of the difference between the terms *Major* and *Perfect* will be had later. Take it on faith just now.

Let us write the Normal Intervals in the Scale of C Major, giving their name and kind. Then play them and endeavor to recognize them when heard. Let us also count the number of Half-Steps in each.

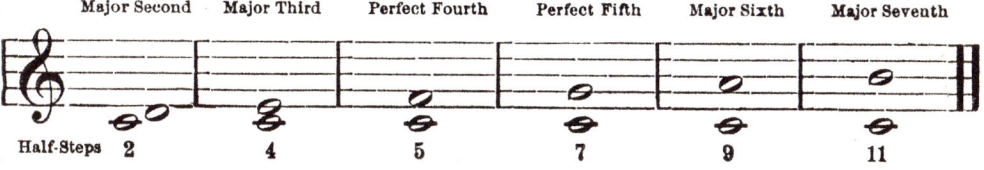

Let the student before going further write out the Normal Intervals in all the other Major Scales in the same manner as above. Do not neglect it; it is well worth doing.

INTERVALS CONTINUED

21

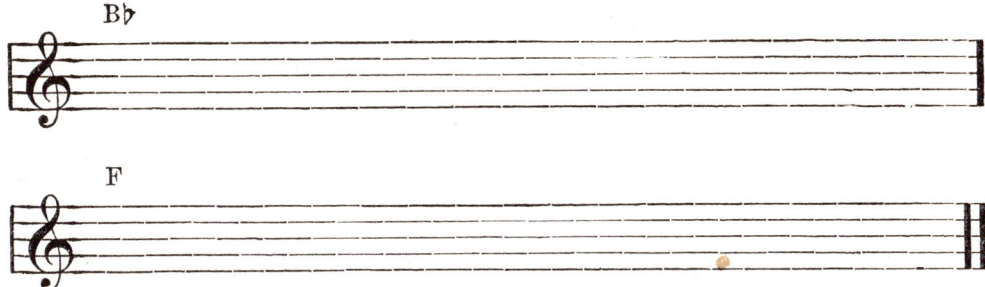

The Normal Intervals should be recognized immediately, and named, in all Major Scales. Practice this.

QUESTIONS AND TESTS

1. Upon what does the Kind or Variety of an Interval depend?
2. What furnishes us with a Standard of Measurement?
3. What are the Normal Intervals?
4. To what Normal Intervals do we apply the term Major?
5. To what Normal Intervals do we apply the term Perfect?
6. How many Half-Steps in a Major Second? In a Major Third? In a Perfect Fourth? In a Perfect Fifth? In a Major Sixth? In a Major Seventh?
7. Give the Name and Kind of each of these Intervals:

CHAPTER VII

FURTHER CONSIDERATION OF INTERVALS

As we all know, the term *Major* means *greater*. Hence, whenever there is a major interval of any name, it stands to reason that there must be a corresponding *Minor* or *lesser* interval of the same name. As stated before, the normal second in the Major Scale is a Major Second:  , having Two Half-Steps. The Minor, or lesser second, then, will have but One Half-Step, hence we write C, D♭, thus:—

 . We could not write C, C♯, as this would not be a second, not including two letters.

Let us treat similarly the Major Third. The Major Third from C would be E: , having Four Half-Steps. Make it Minor and we have:  having Three Half-Steps.

Similarly, let us take up Sixths and Sevenths. Here they are:

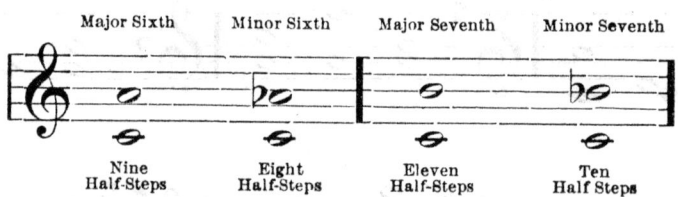

The student should play, then memorize these Intervals. Make an ear test of them also.

We are now ready for a writing exercise: Write Major and Minor Seconds, Thirds, Sixths and Sevenths in the Scales of G, F, B♭, indicating the number of Half-Steps in each.

Half-Steps

Half-Steps

Half-Steps

FURTHER CONSIDERATION OF INTERVALS

We have stated that Normal Fourths and Fifths are called *Perfect;* hence the terms Major and Minor do not apply.

But if we lessen a Perfect Fourth (or Fifth) by One Half-Step, we call it a **Diminished Fourth** (or **Fifth**) and if we increase a Perfect Fourth (or Fifth) by One Half-Step, we call it an **Augmented Fourth** (or **Fifth**).

EXAMPLE:

Try these Intervals and listen closely.

Now the student should write Perfect, Diminished and Augmented Fourths and Fifths in the Scales of G, D, A, indicating the number of Half-Steps.

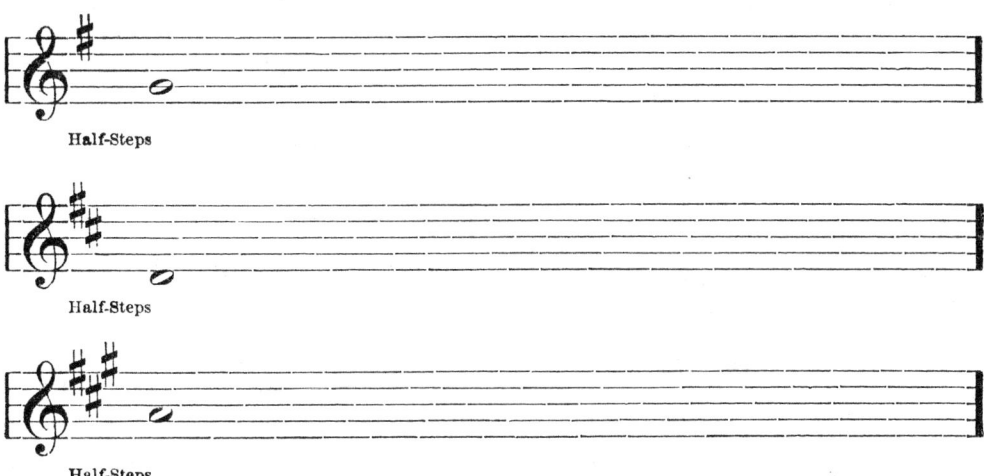

Remember, that the *number of letters included* to make any Interval must always be correct, no matter how we may be obliged to employ Sharps, Flats, etc., in order to attain the proper number of Half-Steps. Here are some examples:

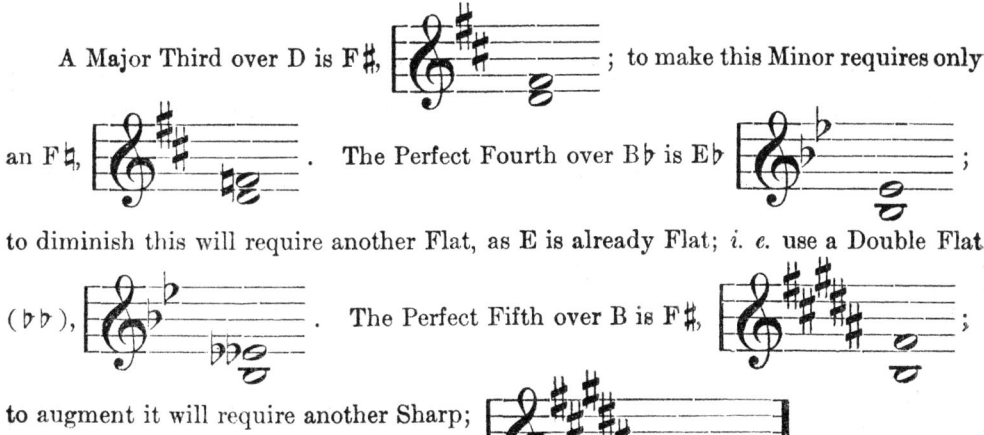

Let the student write the given Intervals in the following Exercise, indicating the number of Half-Steps in each case.

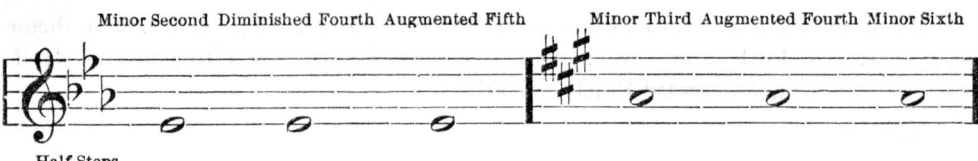

Certain Major Intervals may be further increased. They are then called Augmented. Certain Minor Intervals may be further decreased. They are then called Diminished. For instance:

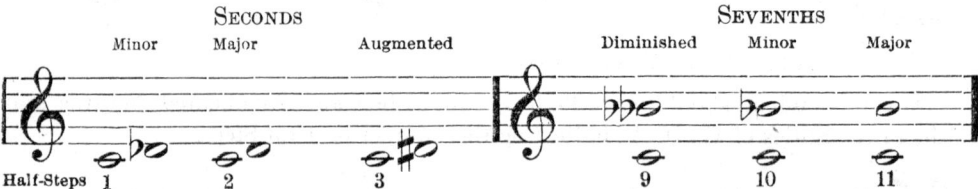

Here is a complete Table of Intervals in the Scale of C, those in ordinary use, omitting purely theoretical ones.

The student must fill up similar Tables in G, D, A, E, B, F, B♭, E♭, A♭, D♭.

FURTHER CONSIDERATION OF INTERVALS

Now let the student write the Name and Kind of each Interval given in the following Exercise. Signatures are omitted purposely.

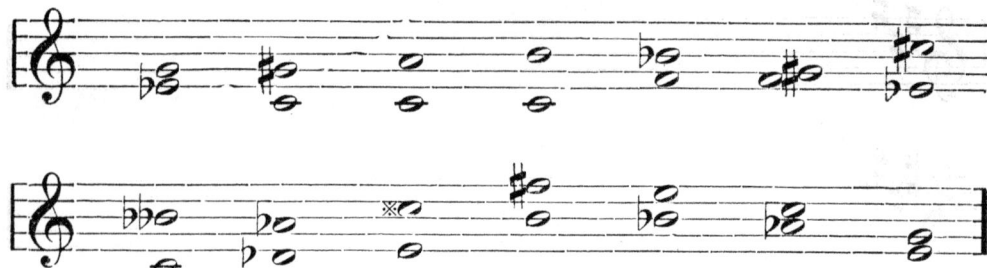

This is an important Exercise. It must be worked out correctly.

Intervals may be **Inverted.** By this we mean that the notes change their relative positions. For instance: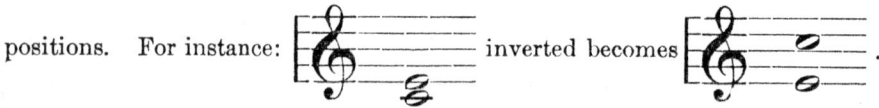

Let the student experiment for himself. In the following Exercise, write out after each given Interval its Inversion:

Examining the above we find that the Inversion of a Second produces a Seventh; of a Fourth, a Fifth; and *vice versa.* We find also that any Interval and its Inversion added together produce an Octave. Inverting a Major Interval produces a Minor; a Minor, a Major, etc.; but inverting a Perfect Interval produces another Perfect Interval.

No student should attempt to proceed further until all the Intervals are mastered, but, if the foregoing work has been done faithfully and understandingly, the way has been paved for what follows.

QUESTIONS AND TESTS

1. How do we determine the Kind of an Interval?
2. How many kinds of Intervals are there?
3. Name them.
4. How many Half-Steps in each of the following Intervals? Perfect Fifth, Major Seventh, Minor Third, Minor Sixth, Major Third, Minor Seventh, Major Sixth, Minor Second, Augmented Fourth, Augmented Second, Diminished Seventh, Augmented Sixth, Major Second, Diminished Fourth, Augmented Fifth, Perfect Fourth.
5. What is meant by Inverting an Interval? Give Examples:

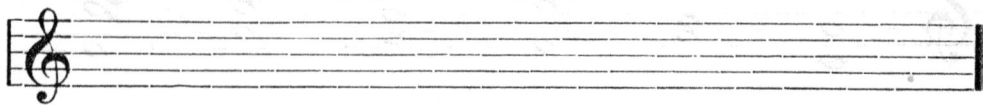

CHAPTER VIII
TRIADS

A **Triad** or **Three Tone Chord** consists of three sounds, namely: the **Root** or **Fundamental**, together with its **Third** and **Fifth**, counting upward, thus:

Play this Triad; each Tone separately, at first; then, all together.

Let the student write upon each degree of the Scale of C a Triad.

Next, write similar series of Triads in each of the following Scales.

Play them all, of course.

Let us number the Triads according to the Degree of the Scale upon which each is found, using the Scale of C as our model, and examine each Triad closely.

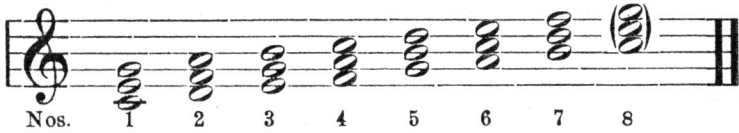

No. 1 consists of Root, Major Third, Perfect Fifth.
No. 2 " " Root, Minor Third, Perfect Fifth.

No. 3 consists of Root, Minor Third, Perfect Fifth.
No. 4   "   " Root, Major Third, Perfect Fifth.
No. 5   "   " Root, Major Third, Perfect Fifth.
No. 6   "   " Root, Minor Third, Perfect Fifth.
No. 7   "   " Root, Minor Third, Diminished Fifth.

It will be observed that the first six Triads all have Perfect Fifths but that the seventh Triad has a *Diminished Fifth*. This latter is known as a **Diminished Triad** because of its diminished fifth. *Remember this always.*

A further examination of the first six Triads discloses the fact that three of them have Major Thirds and three of them have Minor Thirds. Triads which have *Major Thirds* and *Perfect Fifths* are known as **Major Triads**; Triads which have *Minor Thirds* and *Perfect Fifths* are known as **Minor Triads**.

Nos. 1, 4, 5 in any Major Scale are always Major Triads; Nos. 2, 3, 6 in any Major Scale are always Minor Triads.

Play these Major Triads from the Scale of C Major again and again. Try to recognize them when heard.

MAJOR TRIADS IN C MAJOR

Nos. 1   4   5

Compare with these the Minor Triads, Nos. 2, 3, 6.

Nos. 2   3   6

Play these also many times over and learn to recognize them.

Finally play No. 7 with its Minor Third and Diminished Fifth. Note how different from the others and never forget it.

DIMINISHED TRIAD

No. 7

These seven Triads are found in the same form and order in every Major Scale.

Let us write them all out, as before, number and mark them.

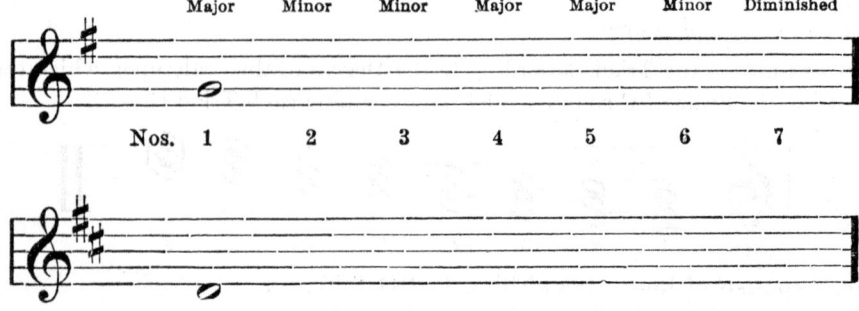

TRIADS

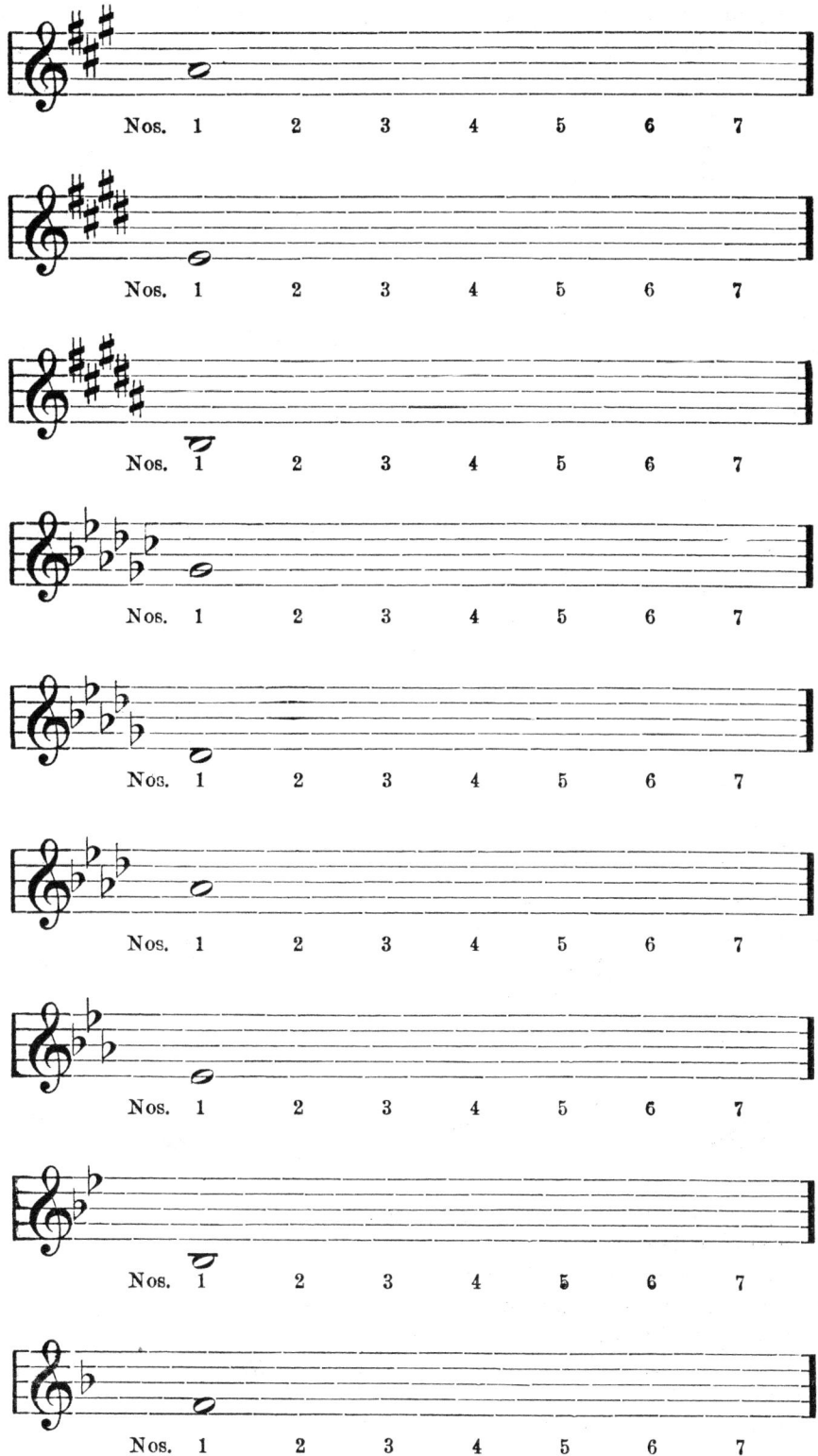

Play them all and mark, as in the first example (Scale of G), which are Major, Minor, Diminished.

Next, analyze the following Triads; indicating by capital letters below the staff the Root of each, and by the abbreviations, Maj., Min., Dim., above the staff, whether the Triads are respectively Major, Minor or Diminished.

Next, build upon each of the given Roots the Triad called for.

QUESTIONS

1. What is a Triad?
2. How many Triads in a Major Scale?
3. How many have Perfect Fifths? Which are they?
4. Which Triad has a Diminished Fifth?
5. Which Triads, having Perfect Fifths, have also Major Thirds? Which have Minor Thirds?
6. How are Triads named?

CHAPTER IX

COMMON CHORDS

Since a Triad is made up of but three different sounds, it follows that if we attempt to write music in four parts, or for four voices, one member of the Triad must be *doubled*, or *used twice*. The best member to double is the Root.

As an example take the C Major Triad:

In this shape it is known as a **Common Chord**.

We may display the Common Chord on two staves, using Treble and Bass Clefs, thus:

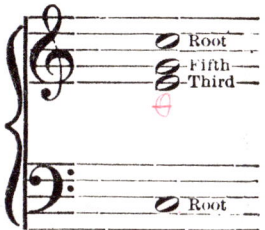

As it now stands, *having the Root in the Bass*, this chord may be written in three **Positions**, thus:

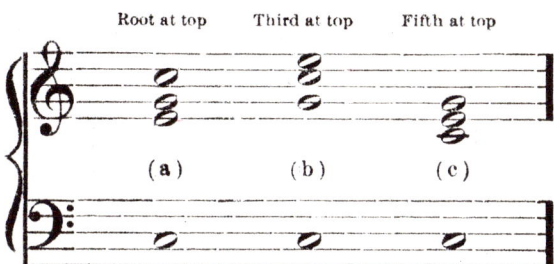

Bear in mind that it is the same chord, no matter how its component **tones may be** moved about.

It is important to recognize these three Positions both with the eye and the ear.

Let us play them. The original position (a), *having the Root at the top*, is known as the **Root Position** or **Octave Position**. In this position the chord has a solid and substantial sound. With its *Third at the top* (b), the chord is said to be in the **Third Position**. This position seems to give an effect of lightness and grace. With its *Fifth at the top* (c), the chord is said to be in the **Fifth Position**. This position seems to indicate something to follow or to ask a question.

Every Common Chord may be treated in this manner.

The student should next write out in full each of the **Six Common Chords** in the Scale of C, using the three positions of each.

As the *Triad* on the *Seventh Degree of any Scale* is *Imperfect*, having a *Diminished Fifth* we will not include it among the Common Chords.

Next, let us try all the Common Chords in the Scale of G, in their three positions:

And similarly in the Scale of F:

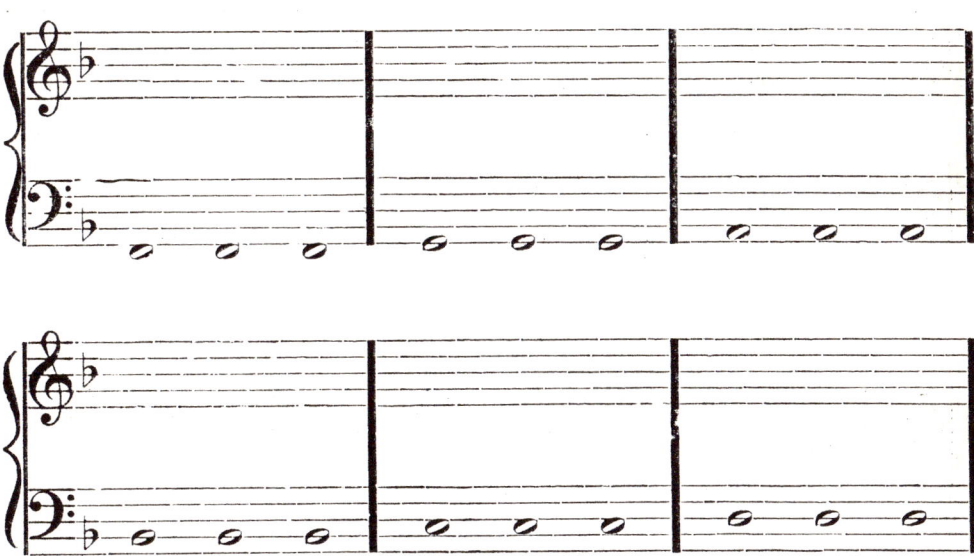

All the preceding exercises should be played over many times in order that the student may become familiar with the effect of each of the Major and Minor Common Chords in their respective positions.

The following exercise is most important. In this case each bass note is the *Root of a Chord*. No signature is given, so the student must supply the necessary sharps or flats in writing each chord. It is indicated whether the chord is to be Major or Minor, and the required Position is also indicated.

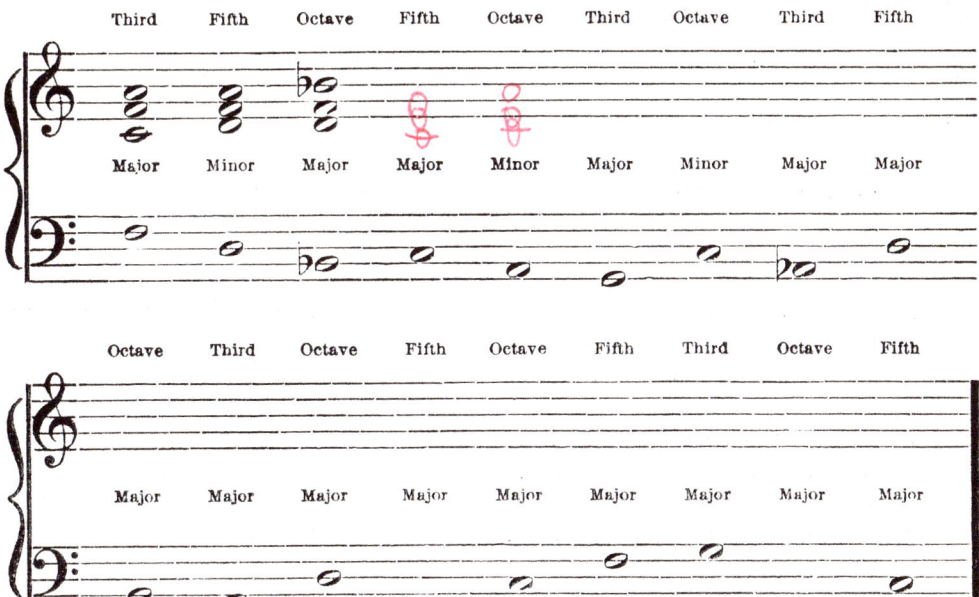

Next, let the student analyze the following, indicating the bass notes by a capital letter under each, writing between the staves whether the chord is Major or Minor, and indicating the Position above the upper staff:

Play each of the preceding chords many times over and listen carefully.

QUESTIONS

1. How do we obtain a Four Part Chord from a Triad, and which is the best way?
2. What is it called when so obtained?
3. In how many Positions can a Common Chord be written? How are they obtained?
4. How are the three Positions of the Common Chord usually named?
5. What may be said as the separate effect of each Position?
6. How many Common Chords may be written in each Scale? Upon what degrees?
7. What of the Chord on the Seventh Degree of the Scale?

CHAPTER X
COMMON CHORDS IN SUCCESSION

We now enter upon the real study of Harmony. All the preceding has been a preparation for and a leading up to this stage. We have learned to build up and to recognize the Common Chord, the backbone of all musical construction, and now we must begin to learn the use of it.

If all the preceding successive steps have not been thoroughly understood and mastered, they should be reviewed again and again. We must go from the known to the unknown, and one step depends upon the other.

We are now to learn the use, in *Succession*, of the Six Common Chords in any Major Scale, each chord having its Root for a Bass Note.

For our present purposes the following may be presented as a good working Principle:

Do not write two Common Chords in succession. each having the same Position.

EXAMPLES:

In examining the preceding Example, it will be noted that at (a) the Common Chord of C in the Octave Position is followed by the Common Chord of G, also in the Octave Position. At (b) the awkwardness of such a succession is corrected by the use of the Common Chord of G in the Third Position. At (c) two Fifth Positions appear in succession. Note how much better the same Chords sound as written at (d). *Train the ear as well as the eye.*

Just another Principle: **Notes common to two chords written in succession should be retained in the same parts or voices, wherever convenient.**

A study of the following example will make this Principle clear:

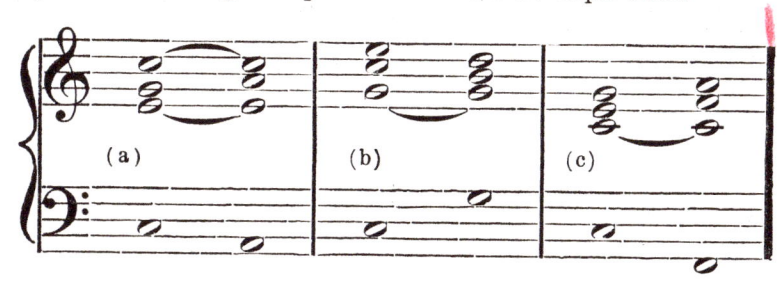

At (a) C is the Root of the C Major Chord and the Third of the A Minor Chord; it is retained in the upper voice. E is the Third of the C Major Chord and the Fifth of the A Minor Chord; this note is also retained in the same voice. At (b) G is common to both chords. At (c) C is common to both chords.

Here is an example of a given Bass harmonized in accordance with the two foregoing Principles:

POSITIONS:

(musical example with positions: Octave, Fifth, Octave, Fifth, Octave, Fifth, Third, Fifth, Third; with (a) marked; Roots: C F D G E A D G C)

In playing this example do not observe the *Ties* (⌣). These are simply used to indicate the employment of notes common to two successive chords. It will be observed that no two chords are used in succession in the same position. Notes common to two successive chords are retained, except at (a).

The following exercises should be harmonized by the student. Write out each exercise complete, then try it over and listen carefully. It should conform to the foregoing Principles and it *must* sound well. If it is not satisfactory, do it over again. Remember that each Bass Note given is to be the Root of a Common Chord; no two Chords are to be used consecutively in the same Position; retain, as far as convenient, notes common to two successive chords in the same parts or voices.

The Root in the Bass decides *what Chord* shall be used, the student must decide *what Position* is best. In the latter case something is left to the taste and judgment of the individual. What does not sound well should not be written.

Now for some real constructive work.

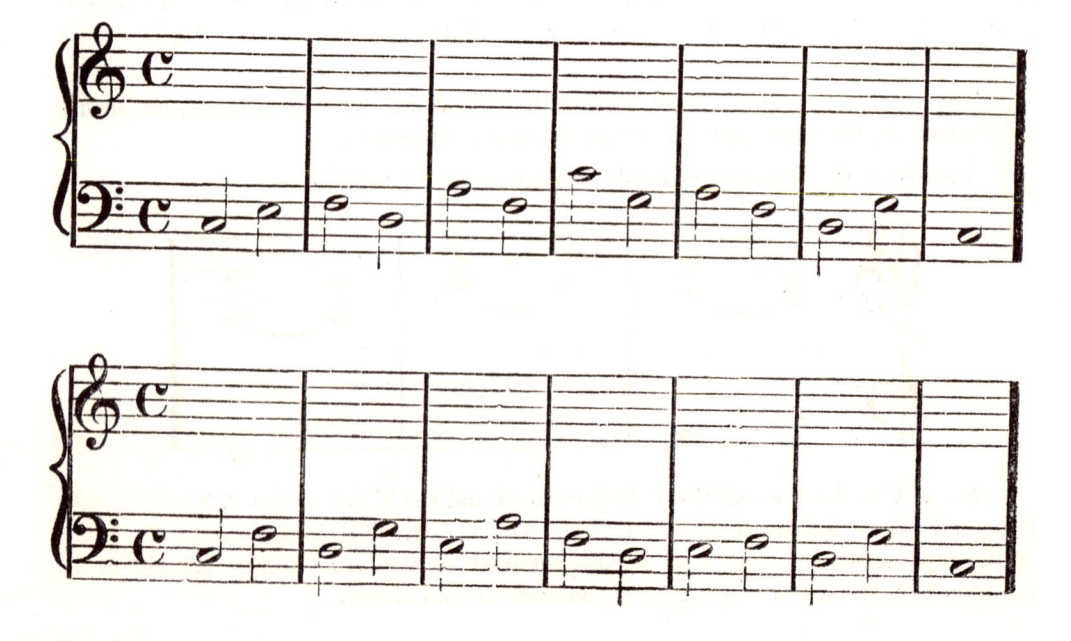

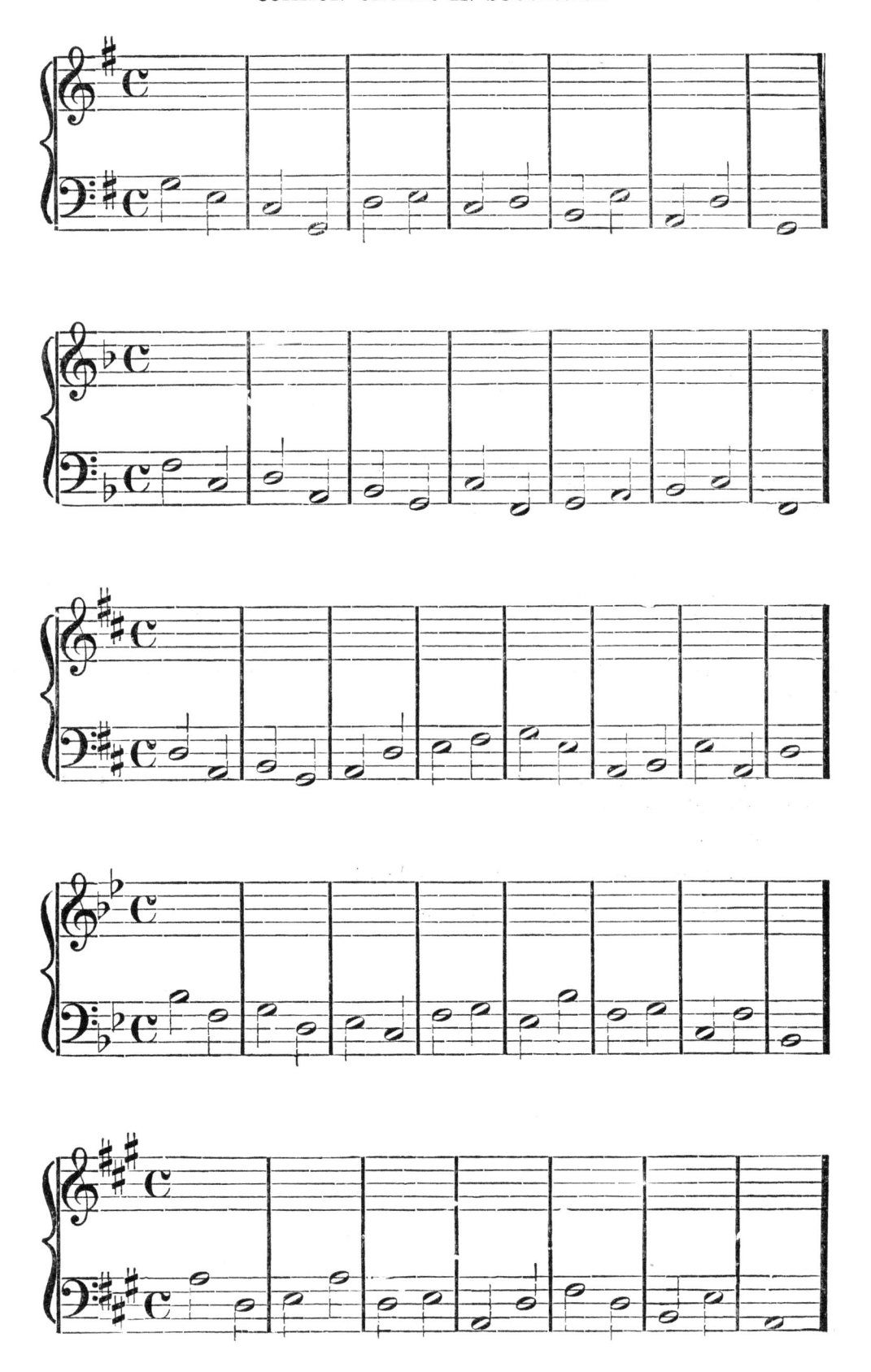

COMMON CHORDS IN SUCCESSION

The Position of the first chord in each of the foregoing exercises has been left to the student. It is suggested that for the sake of practice each exercise be written out three times on a separate sheet of paper, beginning each time with a different position of the opening chord. Then play all three versions in each case and select the one that sounds best.

QUESTIONS

1. What is the first Principle to be observed in writing Succession four-part Common Chords with the Roots in the Bass?

2. What is the next Principle?

3. How do we know what Chord shall be used?

4. How do we decide what Position to use?

CHAPTER XI
HARMONIZING A MELODY

The knowledge gained in the preceding chapter may be applied to the harmonization of a **Melody**, or upper voice part. To a given bass part we have been adding three other parts or voices. If we examine the various exercises we will find that each note of the topmost part or voice in each exercise is either the Root, the Third or the Fifth of a Chord. This gives the clue to our reasoning.

In harmonizing a Melody we must decide each note as we come to it: whether it is to be the Root, the Third, or the Fifth of a Chord. The Melody Note, for instance, might belong to either of the three following chords:

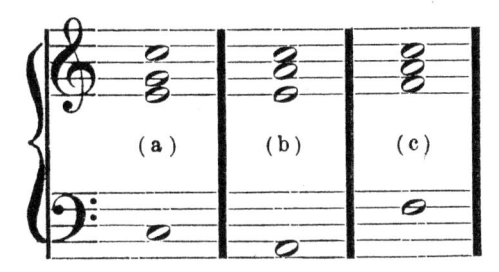

At (a), it is the Root of the Chord C-E-G; at (b), the Third of the Chord A-C-E; at (c), the Fifth of the Chord F-A-C. Play each of these many times and compare the effects. Learn to recognize each one when heard.

Let us take , the Second Degree in the Scale of C. It might be the Root of the Chord D-F-A, or the Fifth of the Chord G-B-D, but it should not be used as the Third of the Imperfect Chord B-D-F.

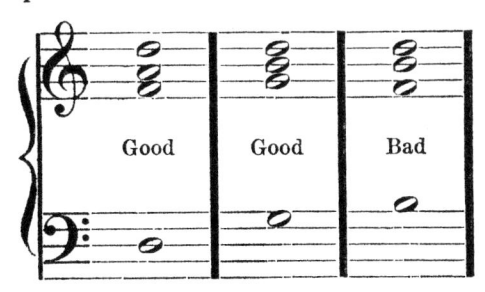

The remaining Degrees in the Scale of C may be harmonized in a similar manner as follows:

It will be observed that F is used as the Root of the Chord F-A-C, and the Third of the Chord D-F-A, but not as the Fifth of the Imperfect Chord B-D-F; B is used as the Third of the Chord G-B-D and the Fifth of the Chord E-G-B, but not as the Root of B-D-F. Make an ear-training exercise of the preceding, listening carefully to the Positions and their effects.

In a manner similar to the preceding let the student write out in full the harmonies for the Scale of G:

And for the Scale of F:

In harmonizing a Melody according to the knowledge so far attained, the Principles of the preceding chapter will be applied, as well as the following.

Each Exercise should begin and end with the Tonic Chord, *or Chord built upon the First Degree of the Scale.*

Place the Root of each Chord in the Bass.

Do not employ the Seventh Degree of the Scale as the Root of a Chord.

Avoid awkward or long skips in the Bass.

Let us work out a harmony for the following:

The first chord must be the Tonic Chord. Put the Root C in the Bass and fill in the chord:— This will also be the final chord.

Having used the Octave Position for the first chord, the next chord should be in either the Third or the Fifth Position. If B is considered the Third of a Chord, the Root of the Chord must be G; if B is the Fifth of a Chord, the Root will be E.

Try both: Since it will have two tones in common with the opening chord let us select the Chord of E, (Fifth Position).

Next, we have C again. This may be the Root of the Chord of C or the Third of the Chord of A:— Let us select the latter.

Next we have D, which may be harmonized:— We prefer the latter.

The next note E may be a Root or a Third. Try these:— [musical example] or [musical example] We incline to the latter.

The next note F may be a Root only. It cannot be a Third, since the preceding Chord has been used in the Third Position. It cannot be a Fifth since the Root would be B and the Chord an imperfect one. It must be:— [musical example] Since we have used F in the Octave Position and we already know that the final Chord is to be in the Octave Position, there is only one thing left for the next to the last note D. It must be in the Fifth Position, thus:— [musical example] Now write out the exercise complete and play it many times, dwelling upon each Chord. This will repay the most painstaking study and repeated analyses.

[musical example]

In Class work, wherever possible, it would be well to sing over this exercise and all succeeding ones, in four-part harmony.

Now let the student try a few.

[musical example]

Stick to the foregoing until it sounds well. **Try it first on a separate piece of paper before writing it in the book.**

Now try another:

See that the Bass part moves easily and naturally. *It must always do so.*

Now one more:

QUESTIONS

1. After harmonizing a given Bass by adding three upper parts or voices, of what members of chords do we find the topmost part or voice to consist?

2. What principles must be followed in harmonizing a given Melody, each Bass note being the Root of a Chord?

3. What is meant by the *Tonic Chord?*

CHAPTER XII
HARMONIZING A MELODY CONTINUED

The **Bass** or *lowest part* and the **Melody** or *topmost part* are known as the **Outer Voices**.

When both Outer Voices move in the same direction, up or down, it is known as **Parallel Motion**; when one Voice remains stationary and the other moves in either direction, it is known as **Oblique Motion**; if the Outer Voices move in opposite directions, it is known as **Contrary Motion**.

EXAMPLES:

In good writing *Contrary Motion is preferable* (where possible); *Oblique Motion is next best; Parallel*, or *Similar Motion is next;* but, **all four parts must never proceed by Parallel or Similar Motion**.

Observe the foregoing Principle in all succeeding work.

Schumann has said that the Bass part should always be as smooth and flowing as the Melody itself. This is a good maxim to bear in mind from the very beginning.

The present work is most vital. It lies at the very foundation of all musical construction. It must be mastered thoroughly before one can go further. Every chord that is written and every succession of chords must be tried out and tested, played or sung, or both. Nothing must be allowed to stand that does not sound well. This is after all, the final test.

The following melodies are to be harmonized in the manner of the preceding chapter with all the old as well as the new Principles in full force.

After having decided what chord to use, *write the Bass Note first*, and then fill in the remaining parts or voices. Look well to the motion of the Bass part.

Occasional Chords and Basses are given as an additional aid to the student in acquiring a smooth and fluent style. The same Chord may be used twice in succession, but the Position should change.

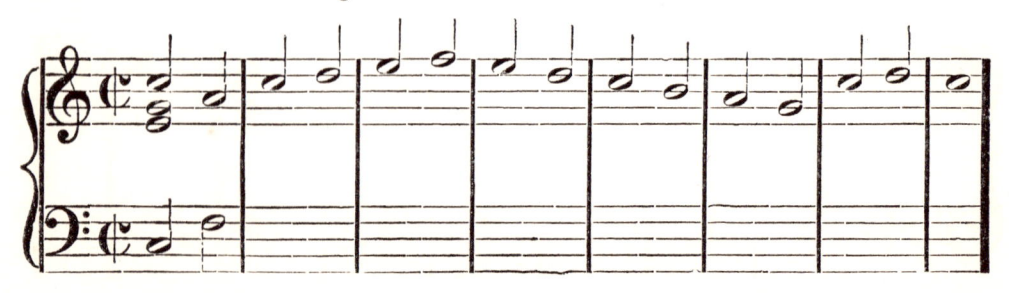

HARMONIZING A MELODY CONTINUED

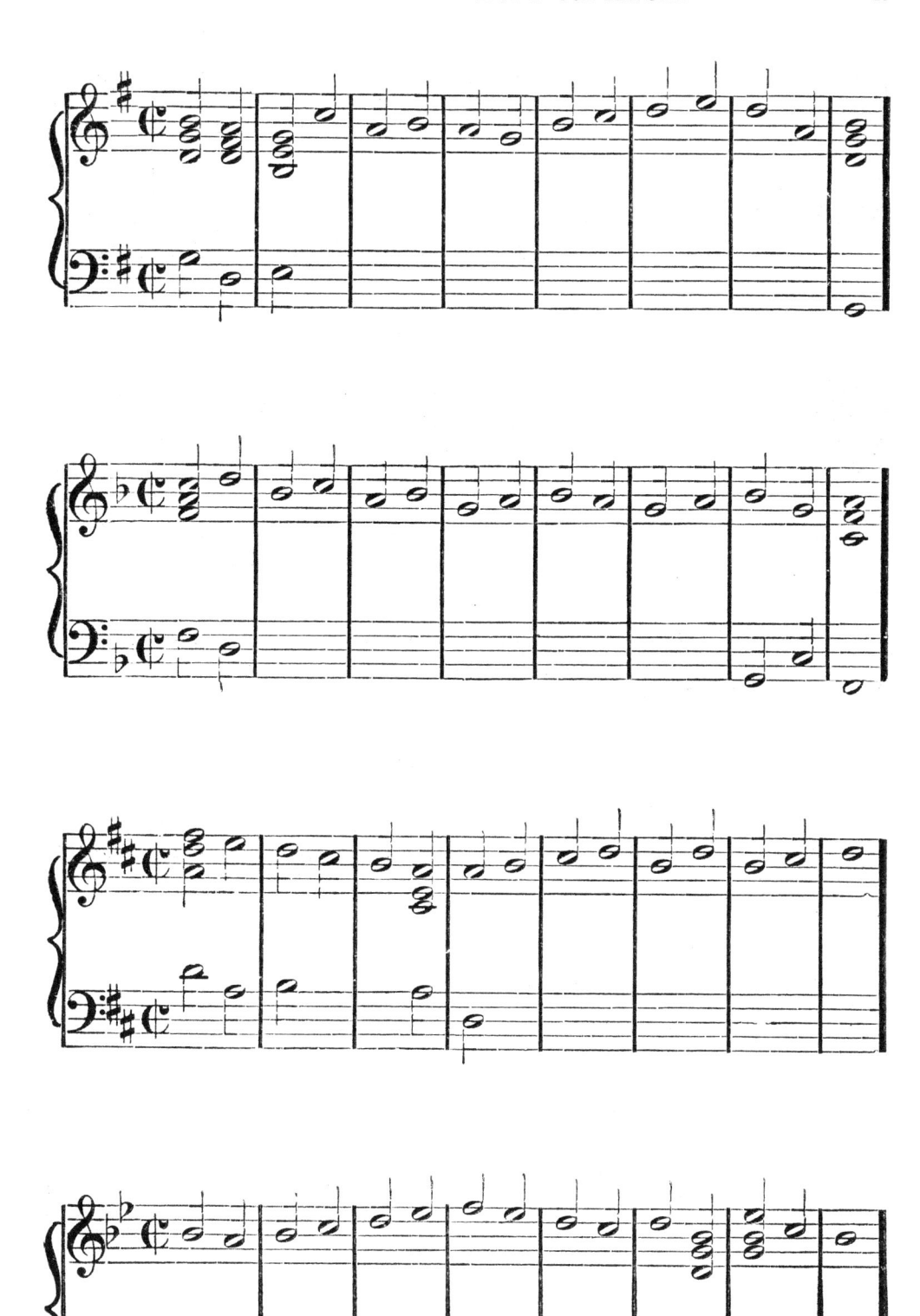

There are further principles and suggestions which serve to aid in the mastery of Successions of Common Chords with Roots in the Bass which must be deferred until later. Temporarily, we must leave the present subject.

QUESTIONS AND REVIEW

1. What are the Outer Voices?

2. What is Parallel or Similar Motion? Oblique Motion? Contrary Motion? Give Examples.

3. Name the above in order of preferences.

4. Give the Principle for the Motion of Voice parts.

5. Make an Example of *all four parts* proceeding in Similar Motion.

6. What did Schumann say about Basses?

CHAPTER XIII

THE FIRST INVERSION

It is not always necessary to use the *Root of every Chord* for a Bass Note. When a Member of a Chord other than the Root is used in the Bass, it is said to be an **Inversion** of the Chord. When the **Third** of any Chord is used in the Bass, the Chord is said to be in the **First Inversion.**

As an example take the Chord of C Major, place the Third in the Bass instead of the Root, and let the Root replace the Third as one of the Upper Voices, thus:

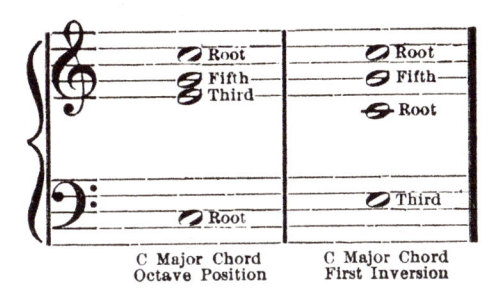

In the following exercise let the student write out, in the same manner, the Octave Position of each Chord in the Scale of C and follow it in each case by the *First Inversion of the same Chord.*

Play these many times contrasting the Position with the Inversion. Train the ear, so that the Inversion may be readily distinguished whenever heard.

Let the student analyze the following exercises, writing above each Chord its Name, and its Position or Inversion.

48 OREM'S HARMONY BOOK

THE FIRST INVERSION

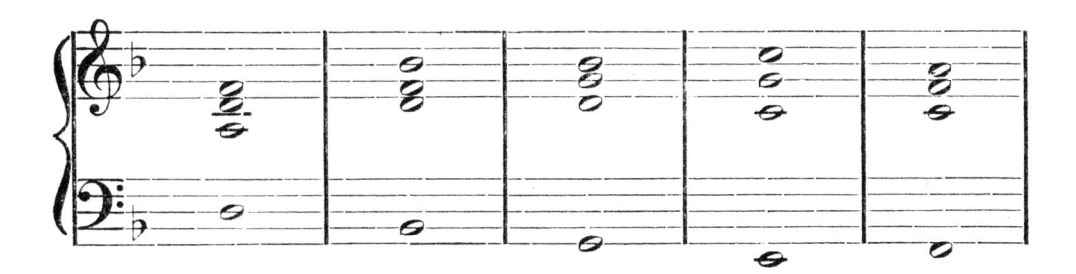

In the **First Inversion of a Common Chord** either the **Root** or the **Fifth** may be doubled (used twice).

To recapitulate, we give below the Positions of the Chord of C, and the various ways in which the First Inversion may be written.

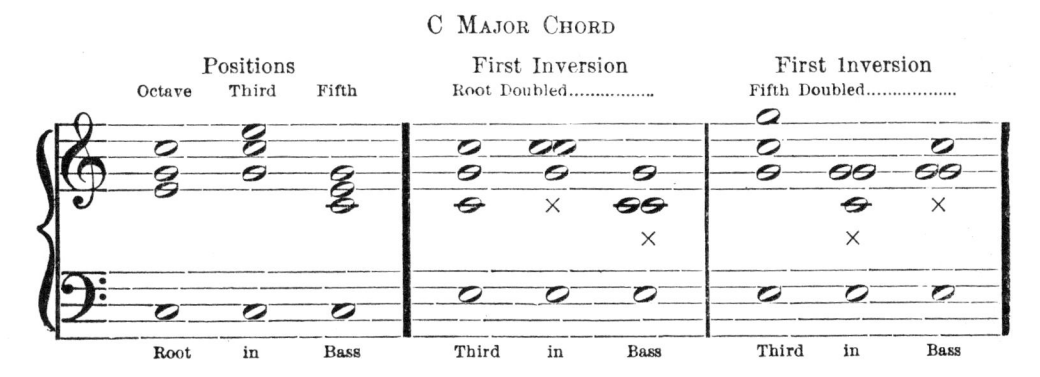

C Major Chord

Positions	First Inversion	First Inversion
Octave Third Fifth	Root Doubled............	Fifth Doubled............
Root in Bass	Third in Bass	Third in Bass

At the Chords marked × it will be noted that the doubling is in unison, both parts or voices taking the same tone. One often sees this in hymn tunes or in other music for four voices.

OREM'S HARMONY BOOK

The foregoing offers abundant opportunity for analysis and ear-training. See what may be done with a single chord.

Now let the student harmonize the following exercises.

Each note marked × is to be the *Third of a Chord;* hence, *a First Inversion* is required. All other notes are Roots of Chords, just as before.

All previous Principles are in full force.

Any *Position* may precede or follow an *Inversion.*

THE FIRST INVERSION

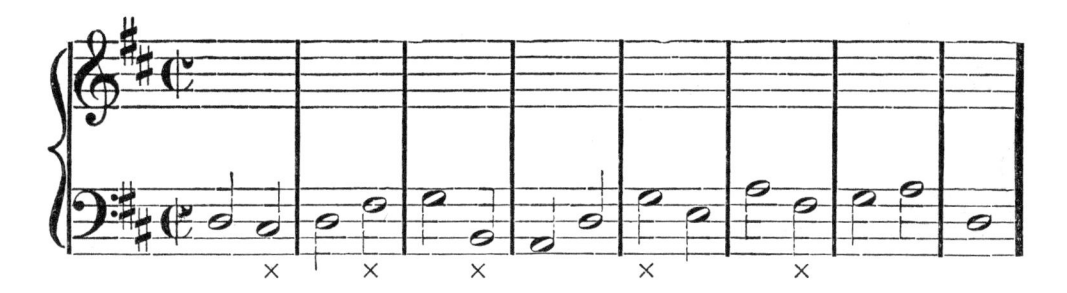

In the following exercises let the student select occasional opportunities to use First Inversions to advantage.

There is one degree of the Scale (*the Seventh Degree*) which, when it is found in the Bass, should invariably be treated as the *Third of a Chord;* since it is not to be used as the *Root* of a Common Chord.

Two First Inversions may be used in succession by doubling the *Root* in one Chord and the *Fifth* in the next; or by doubling in the Unison in one Chord and in the Octave of the next, thus:

Do not consider these exercises as having been conquered until they are made to sound well. Try them again and again.

QUESTIONS

1. What is meant by the Inversion of a Chord?

2. What is meant by the First Inversion?

3. How many Common Chords in any Major Scale may be written in the First Inversion?

4. Which Degree of the Scale *must* be treated as the Third of a Chord?

5. May First Inversions be used in succession? How?

CHAPTER XIV

HARMONIZING MELODIES RESUMED

In a preceding chapter the student harmonized given Melodies, using *Roots of Chords* only in the Bass. At this point the Harmonizing of Melodies may be again taken up and a few First Inversions introduced. More variety may be gained in this manner and awkward places be avoided. A Chord in its *First Inversion* has a certain lightness and freedom which it does not obtain in any of the *Positions*.

Here is an example for Analysis. Let the student indicate in writing the name of each Position and Inversion, giving the Root beneath.

POSITION OR INVERSION:
Fifth Pos.   First Inv.   Third Pos.

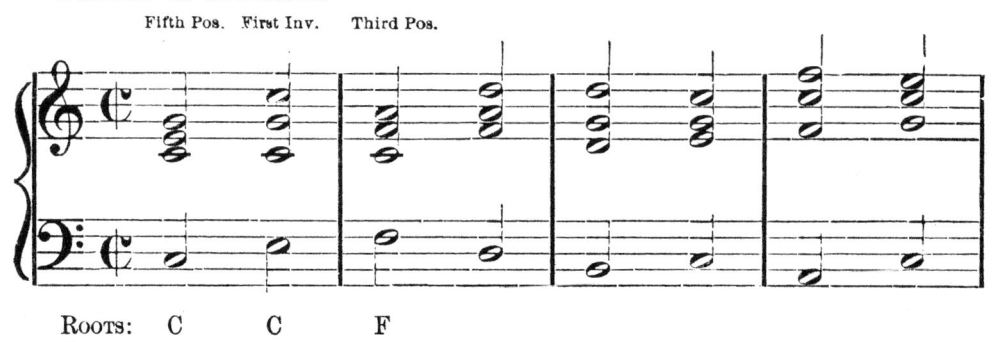

Roots: C   C   F

Using all means so far at his disposal and observing all preceding Principles, let the student now work out effective harmonies for the following Melodies. They must be made to sound well. Strive for good Motion and an easy and melodious Bass.

TONIC CHORD:
First Inv.

No Questions are given at the end of this Chapter, since no new Definitions or Principles have been introduced.

CHAPTER XV
DEGREE NAMES — THE SECOND INVERSION

We have already learned that the **First Degree** of the Scale is known as the **Tonic**, and that the Chord of which the **First Degree** of the Scale is the **Root**, is known as the **Tonic Chord**.

The remaining Degrees of the Scale are named as follows: **Second Degree — Supertonic**, (upon or over the Tonic); **Third Degree — Mediant**, (half way between the First and Fifth Degrees); **Fourth Degree — Sub-Dominant**, (the same distance below the Tonic as the Dominant, or Fifth Degree, is above it); **Fifth Degree — Dominant**, (ruling the Scale); **Sixth Degree — Sub-Mediant**, (half way between Sub-Dominant and Tonic); **Seventh Degree — Leading Note**, (leading to the Tonic). All the Common Chords are named in the same manner, according to the Positions in the Scale of their respective Roots.

The following Exercise is splendid practice.

In the numbered spaces following, let the student write out the corresponding Chords as here prescribed, using the proper Position or Inversion and supplying any necessary Sharps or Flats. The first few Chords are given to show how the remainder are to be filled in.

1. Tonic Chord   — Scale of C — First Inversion.
2. Dominant Chord   — " of C — Octave Position.
3. Sub-Dominant Chord — " of C — Third Position.
4. Mediant   "   — " of G — First Inversion.
5. Sub-Mediant   "   — " of C — Fifth Position.
6. Supertonic   "   — " of G — Third Position.
7. Sub-Dominant   "   — " of F — Octave Position.
8. Tonic   "   — " of B♭— First Inversion.
9. Mediant   "   — " of D — Fifth Position.
10. Sub-Mediant   "   — " of E♭— Octave Position.
11. Dominant   "   — " of A — Third Position.
12. Supertonic   "   — " of F — First Inversion.

In working out the foregoing, reason it out thus: In the Scale of C the Tonic is C; hence the Tonic Chord must be C-E-G, and the First Inversion will require E (the Third of this Chord) in the Bass. In the Scale of C the Dominant is G; hence the Dominant Chord must be G-B-D, and the Octave Position requires G in the Bass and G at the Top, and so on.

At this stage the student should practice diligently the naming and writing of Common Chords according to the Degree names of the Scale.

When the **Fifth of a Chord** is placed in the **Bass**, the Chord is said to be in its **Second Inversion**. In writing the *Second Inversion* of any Chord the **Fifth of the Chord** is the best member to **Double**.

Here is the Second Inversion of the C Major Chord written in three ways, the Fifth being Doubled in each case:

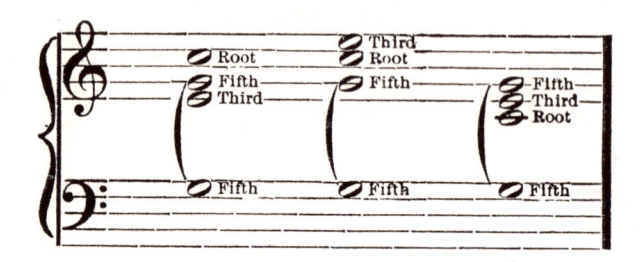

Play these over many times and endeavor to fix the effect firmly in the mind. Note the total difference between the Second Inversion and the First Inversion and how both of these differ from the Positions. Once again let us recapitulate:

C Major Chord:

See what may be done with a single Common Chord. What may be done with one may be done with all.

A Chord in its Second Inversion seems invariably to give the impression of something to follow.

Too much attention cannot be paid to the Second Inversion. Beginners in musical construction, and practical writers also, for that matter, frequently fail to appreciate its significance and true usefulness.

As an exercise let the student write out (each in three ways) the Second Inversions of the Tonic Chords of the Major Scales of C, G, D, A, E, B, G♭, D♭, A♭, E♭, B♭, F, giving the proper Signature for each Scale.

DEGREE NAMES — THE SECOND INVERSION

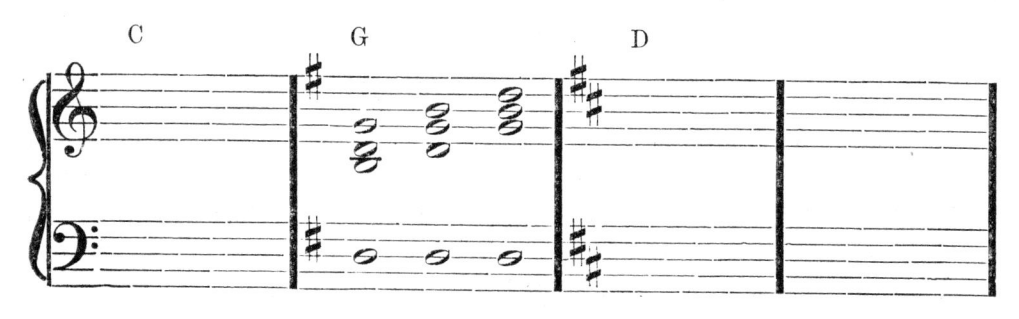

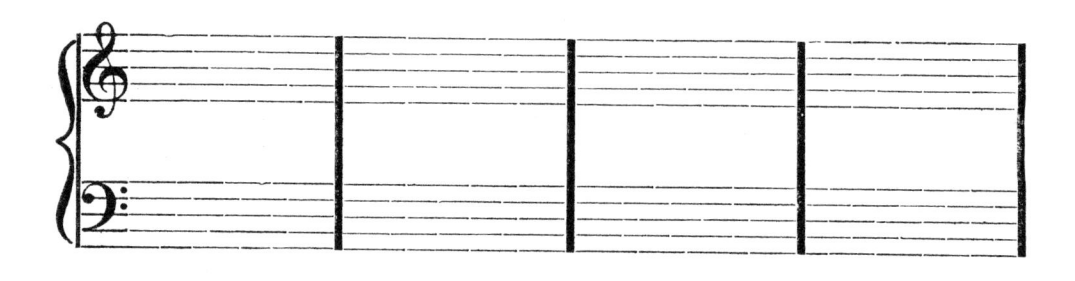

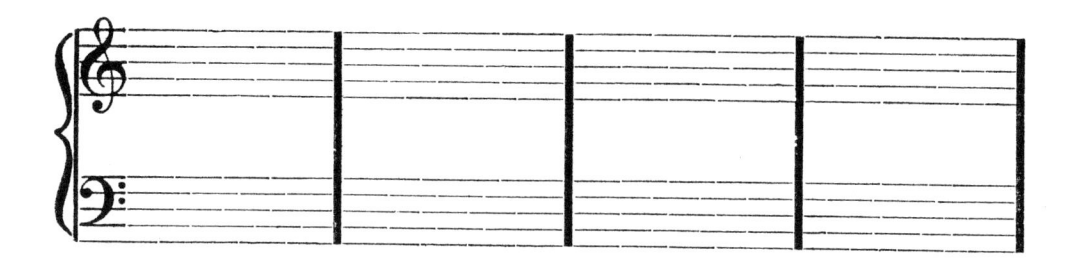

QUESTIONS AND TESTS

1. What names are given to the Degrees of the Scale, in their order?

2. Do these names apply also to the Common Chords based on each Degree?

3. What is meant by each of these Degree Names as applied to its appropriate Degree?

4. What is meant by the Second Inversion of a Chord?

5. In the Second Inversion what member of the Chord is best to double?

6. What is the Dominant Degree in the Scale of C? Sub-Dominant in F? Mediant in A? Sub-Mediant in D? Leading note in G? Leading note in E? Tonic in B♭? Supertonic in B♭?

7. Name the Root, Third and Fifth of each of the following Chords: Tonic, (Scale of G); Dominant, (Scale of D); Sub-Dominant, (Scale of B♭); Mediant, (Scale of A); Sub-Mediant, (Scale of G); Supertonic, (Scale of E).

CHAPTER XVI

SECOND INVERSION CONTINUED

Ordinarily the *Tonic Chord* in any Scale is used most in the *Second Inversion*. In such cases it is best to follow the Second Inversion of the Tonic Chord by the Dominant Chord with its Root in the Bass. For instance: If the Chord C-E-G be used in the *Second Inversion*, having its Fifth (G) in the Bass, it will be followed by G-B-D, (the Dominant Chord in the *Scale of C*) with its Root (G) in the Bass, thus:

SCALE OF C:

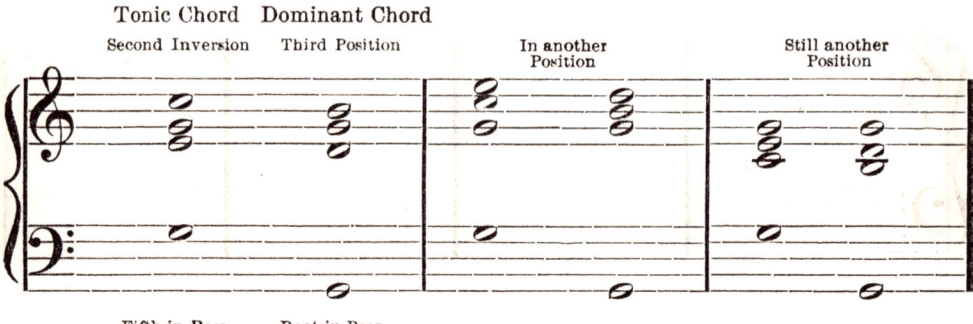

Tonic Chord   Dominant Chord
Second Inversion   Third Position   In another Position   Still another Position

Fifth in Bass   Root in Bass

Make an Ear-training test of the above. It is one of the most common Successions of Chords, and one should be able to recognize it readily whenever heard.

Now let the student write out the above example in each of the Scales indicated, in the spaces given below.

Scale of G.

Scale of F.

SECOND INVERSION CONTINUED

Scale of D.

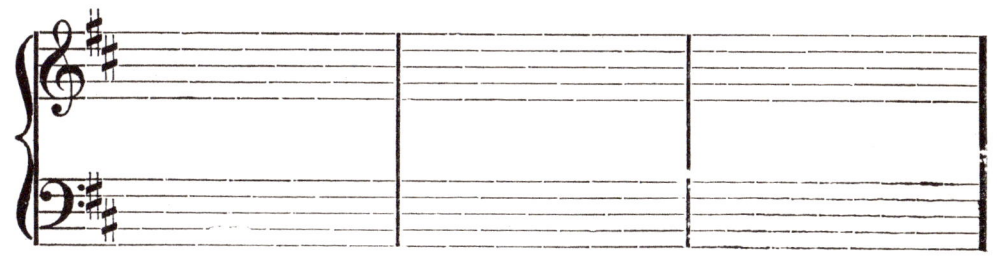

Scale of B♭.

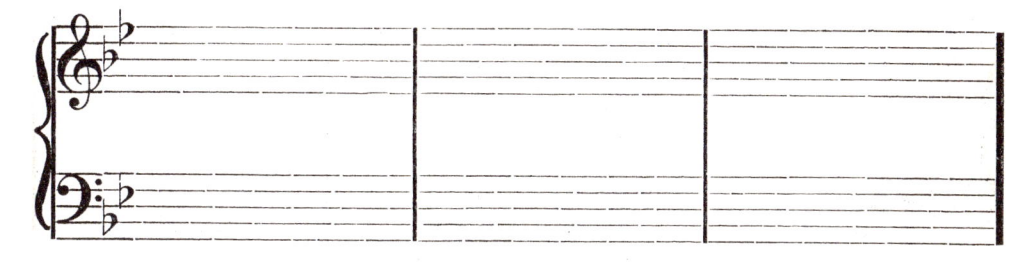

Scale of A.

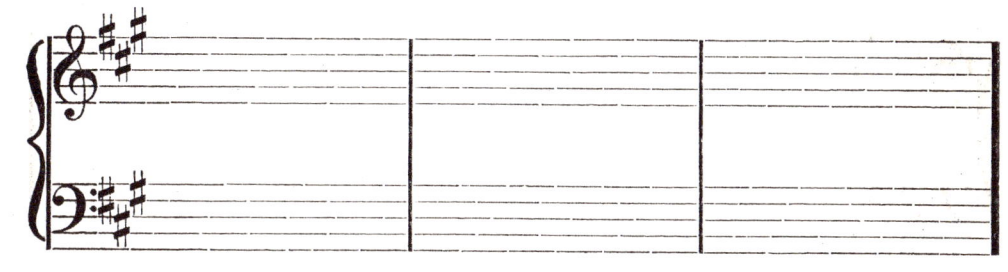

Scale of E♭.

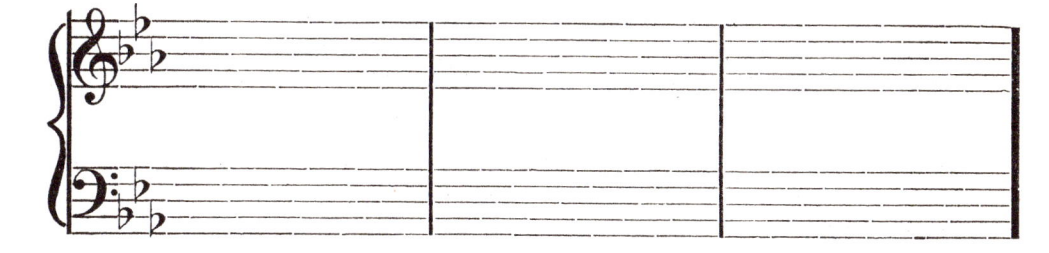

Scale of E.

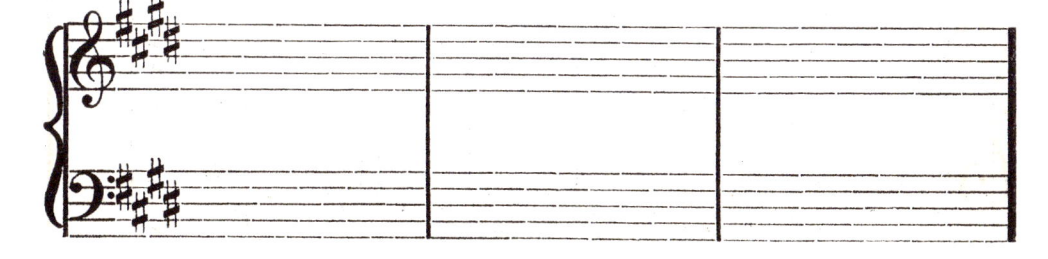

Scale of A♭.

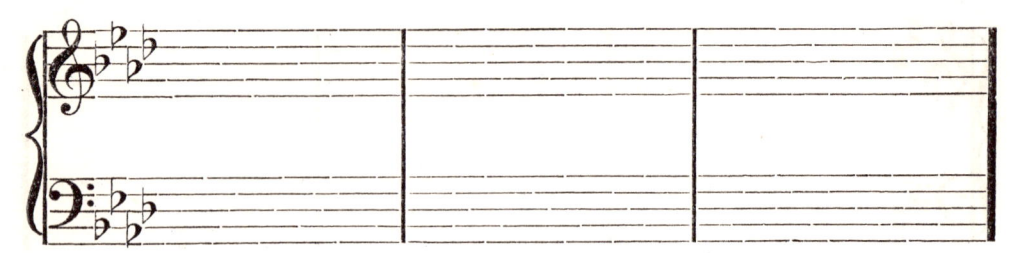

Scale of B.

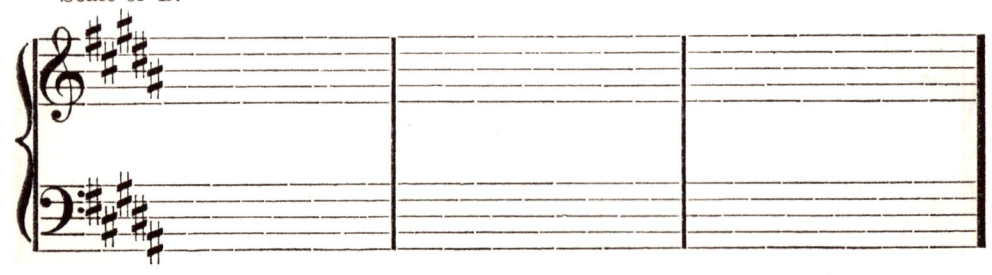

Scale of D♭.

After these have all been written in correctly, play them all, many times over.

The student should now be prepared to employ the *Second Inversion* in the harmonization of some given Basses. In these Basses *First Inversions* should also be employed. Bass notes not marked will be Roots of Chords as usual: notes marked × will be Thirds of Chords, indicating the use of the First Inversion: *notes marked* ⚹ *will be Fifths of Chords*, indicating the use of *the Second Inversion*.

First of all we append a short exercise for analysis by the student. Each Chord is numbered, and upon the corresponding numbered line following the exercise let the student write out just what each chord is, in the manner given for No. 1.

For analysis, by the student.

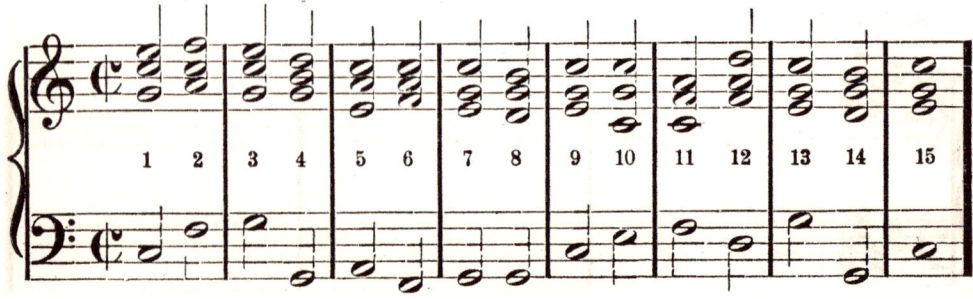

SECOND INVERSION CONTINUED

1. Tonic Chord — Third Position.
2.
3.
4.
5.
6.
7.
8.
9.
10.
11.
12.
13.
14.
15.

Now harmonize the following, as directed on the preceding page.

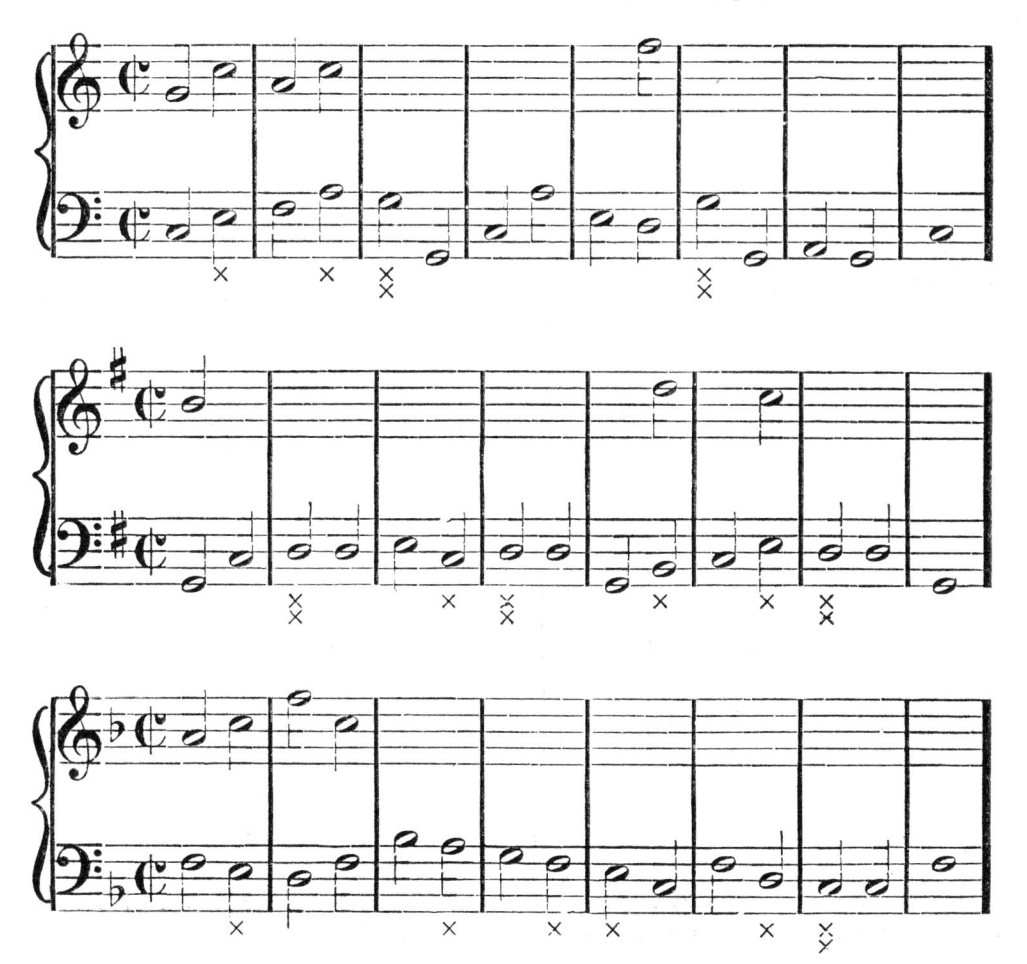

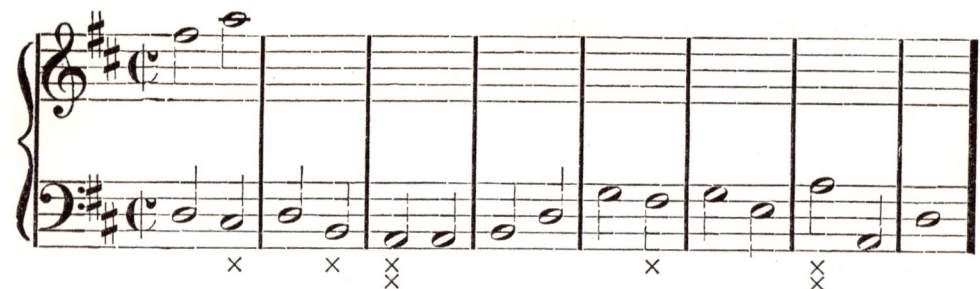

All of the foregoing may be made to sound smooth and melodious. The student *must conquer them* before proceeding further.

In harmonizing the foregoing the student will have discovered that, after all, a Second Inversion is about as easy to manage as anything else.

Whenever the *Fifth of the Scale* is found *twice in the Bass, consecutively*, a *Second Inversion* of the *Tonic*, followed by the *Dominant*, seems to be indicated. Consequently, let the student, who is already familiar with the use of the First Inversion, harmonize the following Basses to suit himself, bearing in mind, of course, that they *must sound well*.

QUESTIONS

1. What Chord is most generally used in the Second Inversion?
2. How is it followed?
3. In harmonizing a Bass, how can an opportunity for use of the Second Inversion of the Tonic be most readily discovered?

CHAPTER XVII
CADENCES

The word **Cadence** (Latin: *cadere*, to fall), as used in the art of music, refers to the form of ending of any musical thought. The word *Cadence* referred originally to the fall of the voice, in spoken language.

The more important musical **Cadences** are as follows:—

Perfect Cadence. The Dominant Chord followed by the Tonic Chord, both chords having their Roots in the Bass, with the final chord in the Root or Octave Position.

EXAMPLE: Scale of C.   Perfect Cadence.

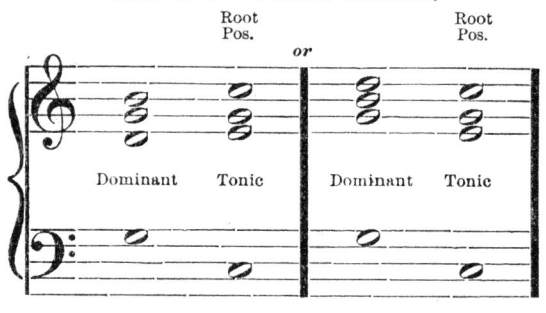

Imperfect Cadence. The Dominant Chord followed by the Tonic Chord, but with either Chord inverted, or with the final chord *not* in the Octave Position.

EXAMPLE: Scale of C.   Imperfect Cadence.

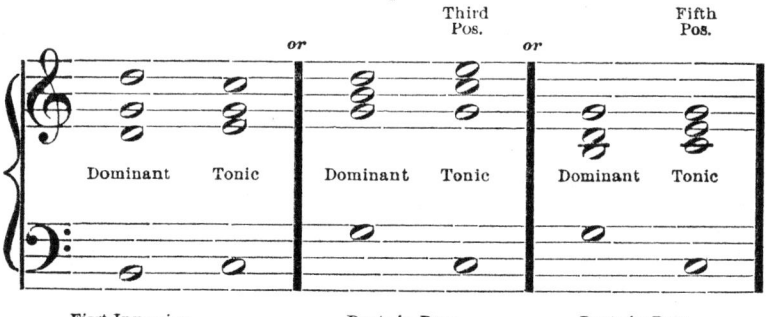

Plagal Cadence. The Sub-Dominant Chord followed by the Tonic Chord (Roots in Bass). An old Church Cadence.

EXAMPLE: Scale of C.   Plagal Cadence.

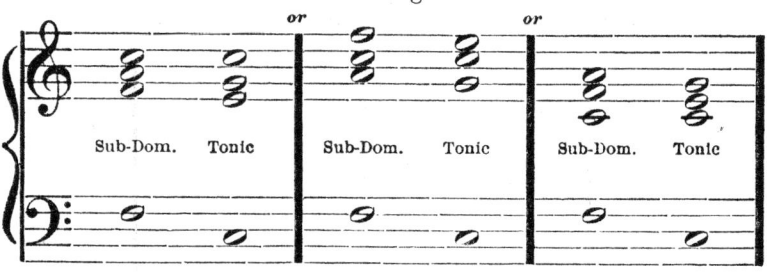

Half Cadence. The Tonic Chord followed by the Dominant Chord (in any Position).

EXAMPLE:

Scale of C.   Half Cadence.

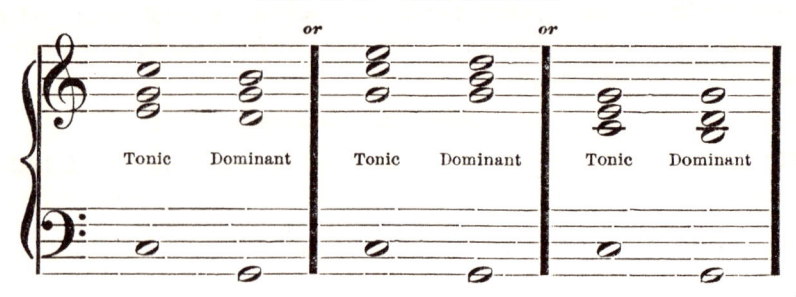

[Musical notation: three pairs of Tonic–Dominant chords, each marked "or"]

Deceptive Cadence. The Dominant Chord followed by any chord, other than the Tonic.

EXAMPLE: Scale of C.   Deceptive Cadence.

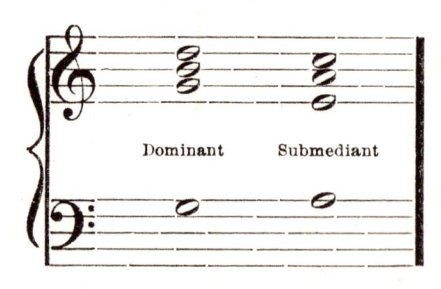

[Musical notation: Dominant–Submediant]

These Cadences all have their uses and a mastery of them will aid the student greatly in harmonizing melodies, in harmonic analysis, and later on, in attempts at elementary composition.

The **Perfect Cadence** implies a *full close;* hence it must be used but rarely, except for this purpose. The **Imperfect Cadence**, while it may be used for a close, is *less final* than the Perfect Cadence; hence it may be employed more freely. The **Plagal Cadence** (*sidewise* or *collateral*), while it is sometimes used for a close, may be employed at will. The **Half Cadence** invariably indicates *something to follow.* It avoids a close. The **Deceptive Cadence** is also used to avoid a close. Both these latter are employed freely.

As an Exercise, let the student write out, in the following given spaces, the **Perfect, Imperfect, Plagal, Half** and **Deceptive Cadences,** in each of the Scales indicated, using all the Positions as given in our Examples for the Scale of C.

SCALE OF G:

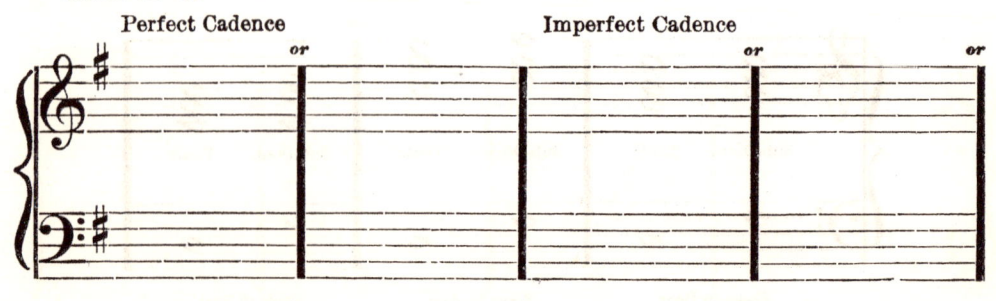

Perfect Cadence   Imperfect Cadence
              or   or   or

[Empty staves for exercises]

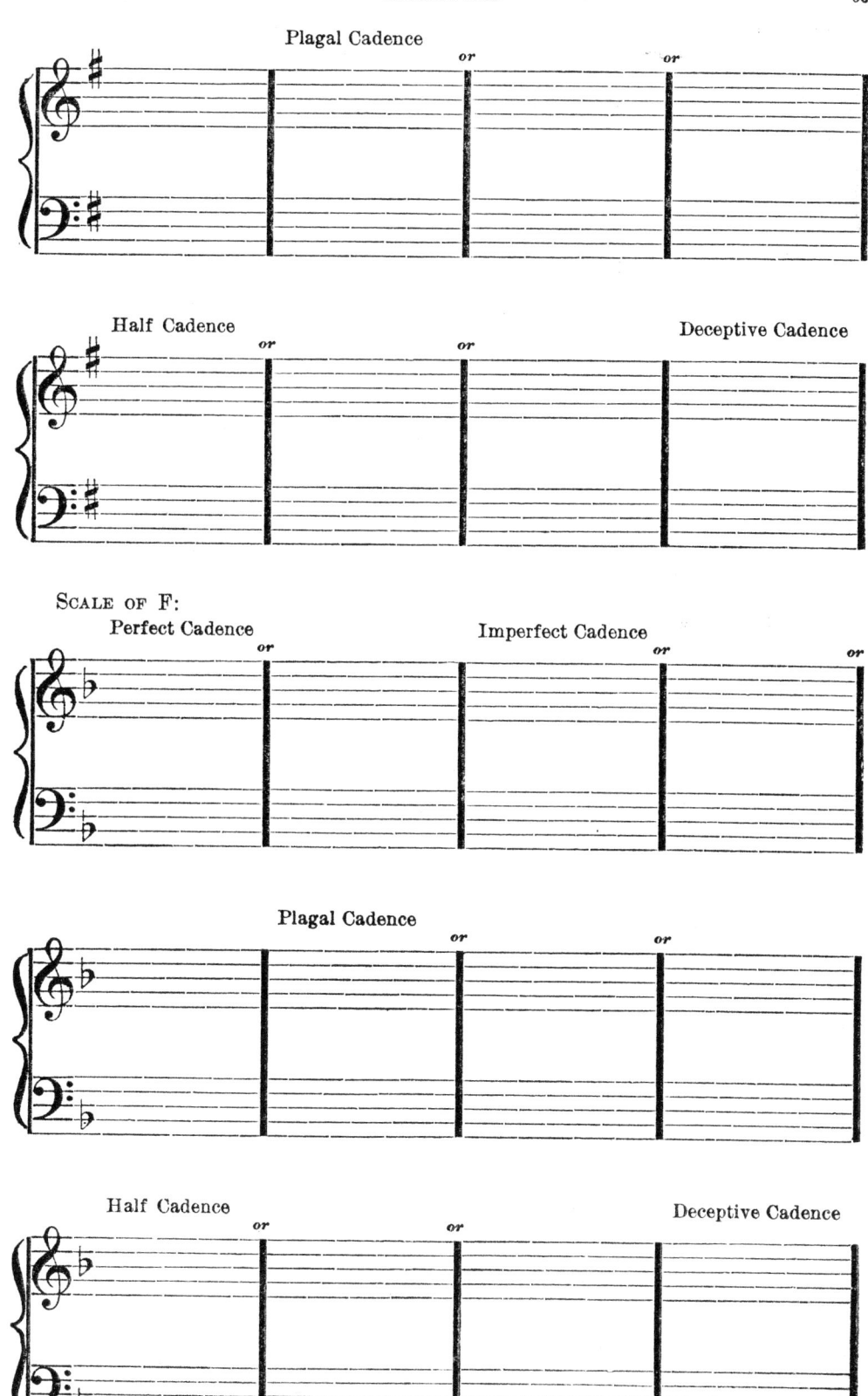

CADENCES

Plagal Cadence   or   or

Half Cadence   or   or   Deceptive Cadence

SCALE OF F:
Perfect Cadence   Imperfect Cadence   or   or

Plagal Cadence   or   or

Half Cadence   or   or   Deceptive Cadence

OREM'S HARMONY BOOK

Scale of D:

Perfect Cadence   *or*   Imperfect Cadence   *or*   *or*

Plagal Cadence   *or*   *or*

Half Cadence   *or*   *or*   Deceptive Cadence   *or*

Scale of B♭:

Perfect Cadence   *or*   Imperfect Cadence   *or*   *or*

Plagal Cadence   *or*   *or*

CADENCES

Half Cadence   *or*   *or*   **Deceptive Cadence**

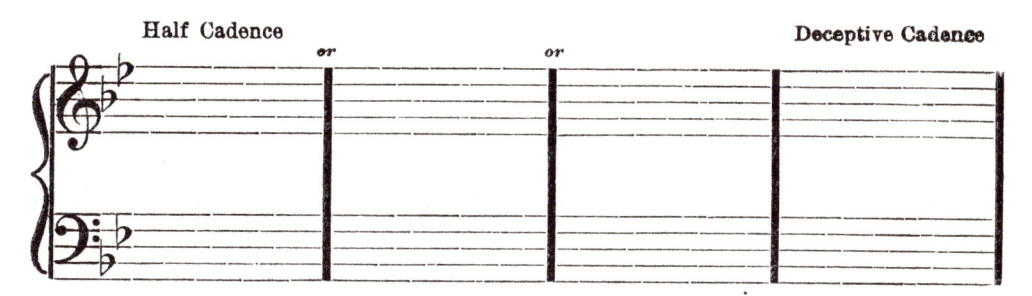

Make Ear-training Exercises of all these.

The student should be able to write out all of the Cadences in any given Scale.

QUESTIONS

1. What is a Cadence?
2. What is the Perfect Cadence?
3. What is the Imperfect Cadence?
4. What is the Plagal Cadence?
5. What is the Half Cadence?
6. What is the Deceptive Cadence?
7. What is the use of each of the Cadences?

CHAPTER XVIII

HARMONIZING MELODIES RESUMED

With all the knowledge so far attained, the student may now essay the harmonizing of some plain melodies. All the preceding Principles are in force. As working tools we have now Common Chords in the Three Positions, First Inversions, Second Inversions, Cadences.

First of all, let us work out together a good, substantial, well-sounding harmony for the following melody. For variety and practice let us work in the Scale of G.

Here is the melody to be harmonized. Let us study it out note by note, numbering each one.

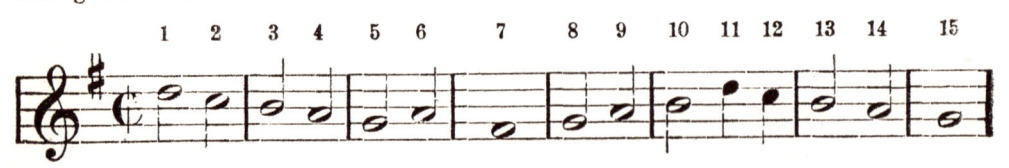

1. We must use the Tonic Chord: G, B, D, preferably with its Root in the Bass.

2. C may be the Root of the Chord C, E, G, or the Third of the Chord A, C, E; but it may not be the Fifth of the Leading Note Chord. Let us select the Chord C, E, G, Root in the Bass (Octave Position).

3. B may not be the Root of the Chord B, D, F♯ since we have used the preceding Chord in the Root or Octave Position; but B may be the Third of the Chord G, B, D or the Fifth of the Chord E, G, B. Let us select the former. This we discover to be the Tonic Chord, and, as a Second Inversion is admissible, let us try one: G, B, D, with D (the Fifth) in the Bass. Bear in mind, however, that we could not have employed a Second Inversion of the Tonic at this Point, had we not, by looking ahead, discovered the possibility of following it by the Dominant Chord.

4. Since we must here use a Dominant Chord, and, as D is the Dominant in this Scale, we know that we must write the Chord, D, F♯, A. Root in the Bass.

5. G may be the Root of the Chord, G, B, D or the Third of the Chord E, G, B; but it could not be used as the Fifth of C, E, G, since that would give us two Fifth Positions in Succession. As the preceding chord is the Dominant let us make a *Deceptive Cadence* by writing E, G, B; E in the Bass.

6. A may be the Root of the Chord, A, C, E, or the Fifth of the Chord D, F♯, A, but not the Third of the Chord F♯, A, C; for two reasons. What are these reasons? Let us make it the Root of the Chord A, C, E, and try a First Inversion, since this will give Contrary Motion between the outer parts. Put C in the Bass and Double A.

7. F♯ may be the Third of the Chord D, F♯, A. If we try this chord, with its Root in the Bass, we will like it far better than B, D, F♯, the only other chord that we could employ.

8. G, the Tonic. A chance for an Imperfect Cadence. Follow the preceding Dominant Chord, by its Tonic, G, B, D, with its Third in the Bass. A First Inversion. Double the Fifth of this Chord in the Unison.

9. A, the Fifth of the Chord, D, F♯, A. Another chance for a Dominant Chord. Put the Root, D, in the Bass.

10. B, Third of the Tonic Chord, G, B, D. Another chance for an Imperfect Cadence. G, B, D, in the Third Position, following the Dominant Chord (D, F♯, A).

11. D may be the Root of D, F♯, A, or the Fifth of G, B, D. Let us select G, B, D, and make it a First Inversion, B, the Third, in the Bass, and D, the Fifth, doubled

12. C may be the Root of the Chord C, E, G; and this is probably the best to use. The Octave Position fits in nicely. Always look out for good motion in the Bass Part.

13, 14, 15. The final chords are always the easiest. Whenever possible, we end with the Perfect Cadence. 14 will give us the Dominant Chord in the Fifth Positon (D, F♯, A; D in the Bass). 15 will give us the Octave Position of the Tonic Chord. Just right. Whenever it may be managed, the Second Inversion of the Tonic Chord is best to precede a perfect Cadence. We have it at 13: G, B, D; D in the Bass; D (the Fifth) doubled. Here is the Exercise completely harmonized, according to the foregoing reasoning.

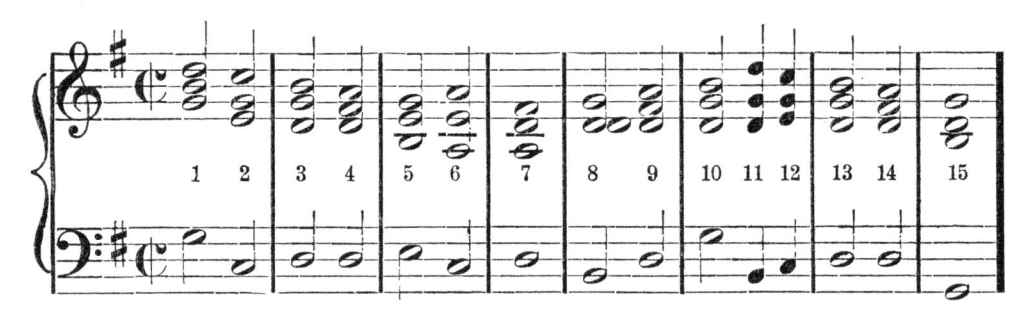

The above will amply repay the closest study and analysis. It is by far the most important thing we have done. This exercise cannot be made to sound better with the means so far at our disposal. The student *must master every detail* of its working out before attempting to go further. Make an ear test of it as well. Play each chord separately, and consider its connection with the chords which precede and follow it.

The student is now ready to harmonize some melodies, reasoning them out and testing by the ear, just as in the preceding exercise.

Here they are.

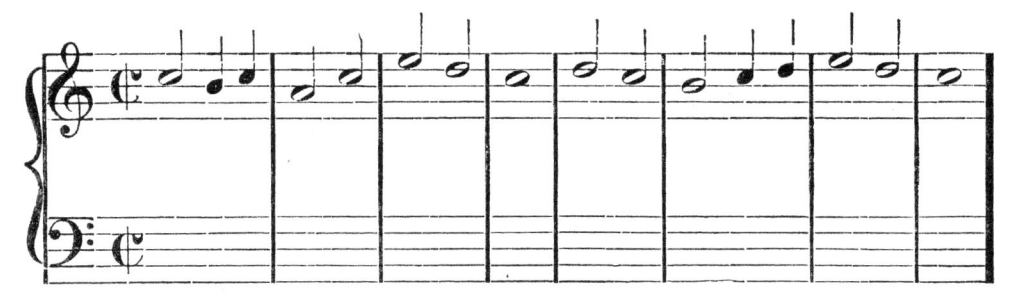

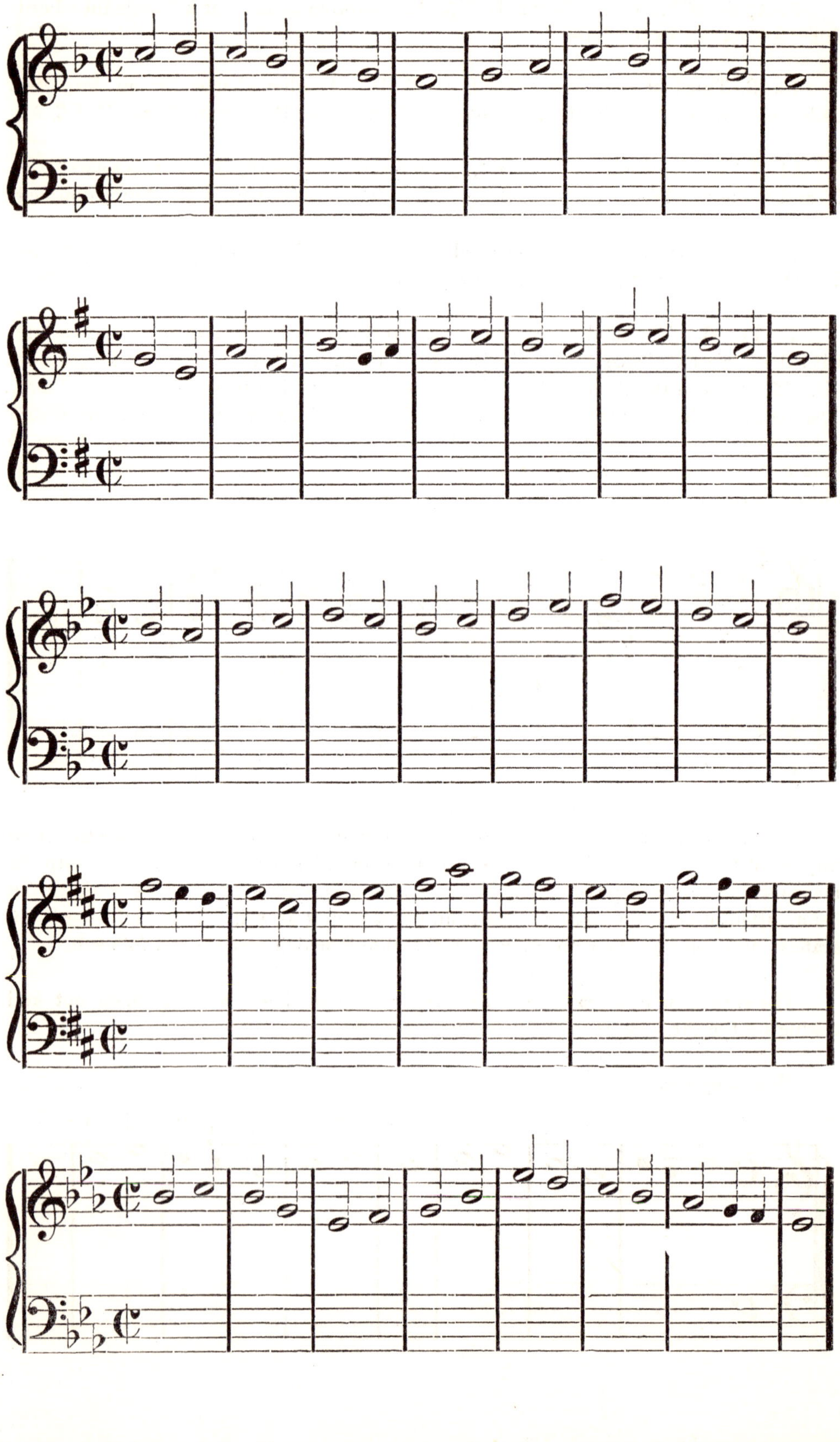

All these must be done, and well done, before the student goes further. Spend as much time as is needed upon this Chapter, and see that every Exercise is made to sound well. All *must* sound well if they are handled properly, according to all the preceding Principles and Precepts.

No Questions are given for this Chapter, since no new material has been introduced, and the work is all of practical character.

CHAPTER XIX
THE MINOR SCALE

So far we have dealt only with the Major Scale. We now come to a consideration of the Minor Scale. As this book has to do only with the practical use of the Scales, as we find them, we will not go into their history. Suffice it to say that each Major Scale is supposed to have a Relative Minor Scale. This relationship lies in the fact that these Scales have many notes in common. The Tonic of the Relative Minor is always found a **Minor Third** below the Tonic of the Relative Major.

Suppose, for example, that we wish to write out the *Relative Minor* of *C Major*. The *Tonic* of *C Major* is C. A *Minor Third* below **C** is **A**; hence, **A** is the Tonic of A Minor. To write out the Scale of A Minor, simply rearrange the notes, just as we find them in **C** Major, starting on **A** as the Tonic. Use the Same Signature for *both*.

Here is the **C** Major Scale:

Now, begin on **A** (a *Minor Third* below *C*) and rearrange these same notes:

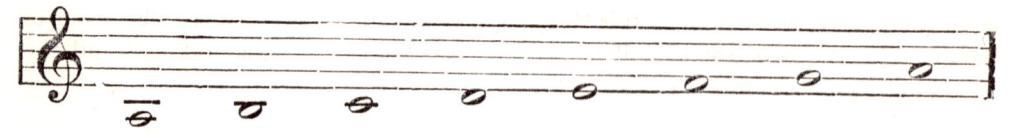

We have now constructed the Scale of **A** Minor.

Let us examine it, play it, sing it, and listen to it.

In this Scale, as it stands, we find the *Half-Steps* to lie between the *2nd and 3rd Degrees*, and the *5th and 6th Degrees*.

SCALE OF A MINOR:

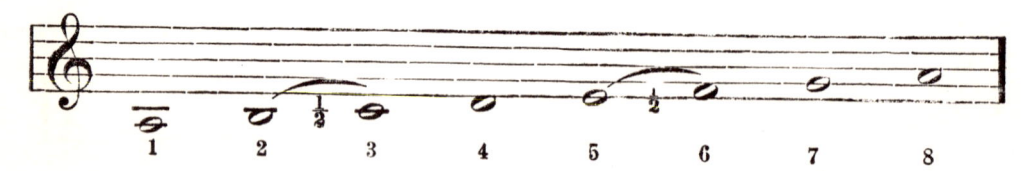

There is little difficulty in recognizing the Minor Scale, when heard; but, for practice, Major Scales and Minor Scales, beginning on various Tonics, should be played and sung, and the student should endeavor to pick them out.

In the form in which we have written it out, the Minor Scale is known as the **Natural Minor Scale**. Modern musical requirements, however, have compelled several modifications in the Minor Scale.

The form of Minor Scale with which we have most to do at present is known as the Harmonic Minor Scale. It differs from the *Natural Minor Scale* only in the fact that the 7th Degree is **raised chromatically** both ascending and **descending**.

THE MINOR SCALE

For example:

A Minor, the *Natural Minor*

A Minor, the *Harmonic Minor.*

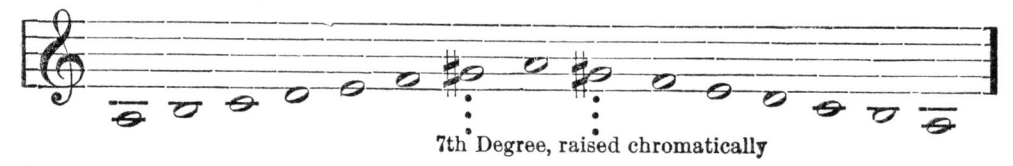

7th Degree, raised chromatically

Play this form, and contrast it with the *Natural Minor;* also, with the *Major*.

There is still another form of Minor Scale known as the **Melodic Minor Scale.** In the Melodic Minor Scale the **6th and 7th Degrees** are **raised** chromatically, ascending, but remain unaltered, descending.

For example:

A Minor, the *Melodic Minor.*

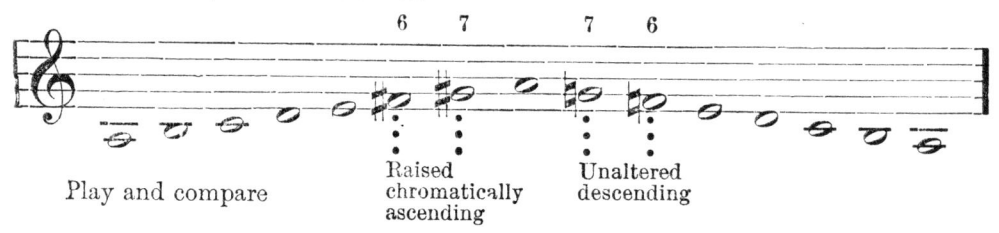

Play and compare — Raised chromatically ascending — Unaltered descending

Now for a most important exercise by the student. Write out in full each Major Scale, as indicated below, giving the proper Signature. Beneath each Major Scale write out in full its Relative Minor; first, the Harmonic Minor; then, the Melodic Minor. Give the proper Signature for each Relative Minor, corresponding with its Relative Major. Make all Chromatic Alterations correctly. In the Melodic Minor use such ♮'s, ♯'s and ♭'s as are necessary to indicate that the 6th and 7th Degrees are to remain unaltered descending.

C Major:

A Minor, Harmonic Minor.

A Minor, Melodic Minor.

G Major:

E Minor, Harmonic.

E Minor, Melodic.

D Major: (write in Signature).

(Name the Scale, and form of Scale), (write in Signature).

A Major:

E Major:

THE MINOR SCALE

B Major:

F♯ Major:

G♭ Major:

Db Major:

Ab Major:

Eb Major:

THE MINOR SCALE

B♭ Major:

F Major:

QUESTIONS

1. What is meant by the Relative Minor Scale?
2. How do you find the Tonic of the Relative Minor?
3. By what name is the original form of the Minor Scale known?
4. How is the Harmonic Minor Scale made?
5. How is the Melodic Minor Scale made?
6. What is the Relative Minor of E♭? Of B? Of D♭? Of F♯?
7. What is the Relative Major of C♯ Minor? Of G Minor? Of F Minor? Of D Minor?

CHAPTER XX

HARMONY IN THE MINOR

As mentioned in the preceding chapter, we have to deal chiefly in this book with the **Harmonic Minor Scales.** Let us investigate the **Triads** in the **Harmonic Minor Scale**, taking *A Minor* as our model. Here they are:

A Minor:

1. The **Tonic,** consisting of Root, Minor Third, and Perfect Fifth, is a **Minor Triad.**

2. The **Supertonic,** consisting of Root, Minor Third and Diminished Fifth is known as a **Diminished Triad.**

3. The **Mediant,** consisting of Root, Major Third and Augmented Fifth is known as an **Augmented Triad.**

4. The Sub-Dominant, consisting of Root, Minor Third and Perfect Fifth, is a **Minor Triad.**

5. The **Dominant,** consisting of Root, Major Third and Perfect Fifth, is a **Major Triad.**

6. The **Sub-Mediant,** consisting of Root, Major Third and Perfect Fifth, is a **Major Triad.**

7. The **Leading Note,** consisting of Root, Minor Third and Diminished Fifth is a Diminished Triad.

Thus, we find, available for Harmony in the Minor, four **Common** or **Perfect Chords** (chords containing *Perfect Fifths*); the **Tonic** (a Minor Chord); the **Sub-Dominant** (a Minor Chord); the **Dominant** (a Major Chord); the **Sub-Mediant** (a Major Chord). Let us make a Table of all our resources, writing out these Chords in their Positions and Inversions. Here it is:

A Minor:

The Tonic Chord.   The First Inversion.   The Second Inversion.

HARMONY IN THE MINOR

The Sub-Dominant Chord. **The First Inversion.**

Root Pos.   Third Pos.   Fifth Pos.

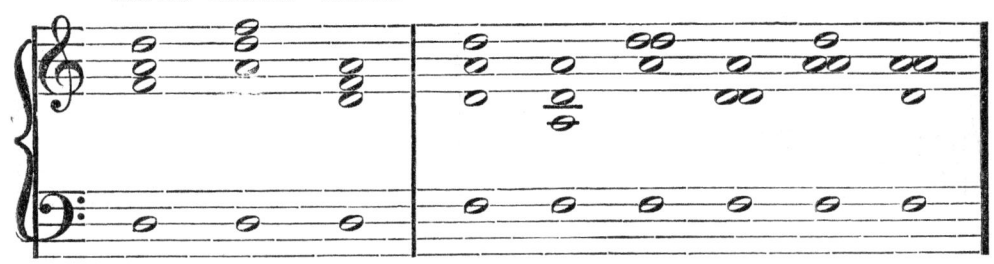

The Dominant Chord. **The First Inversion.**

Root Pos.   Third Pos.   Fifth Pos.

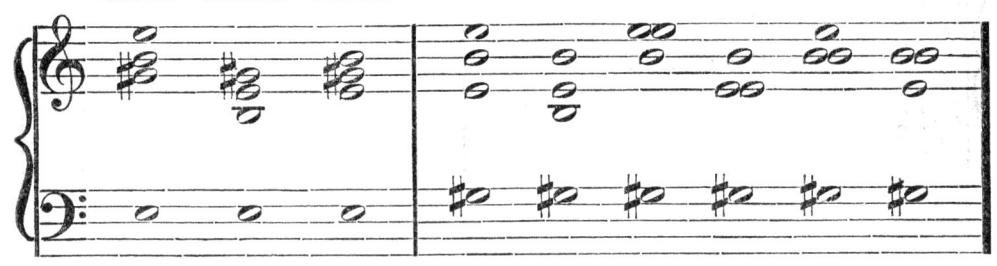

Note the Major Third in this Chord (G♯), obtained by raising Chromatically the Seventh Degree of the Scale.

The Sub-Mediant Chord. **The First Inversion.**

Root Pos.   Third Pos.   Fifth Pos.

Play all of the above examples many times, both Triads and Common Chords. Train the ear, and learn to distinguish one from the other.

Now, let the student write out in the remaining Minor Scales, giving correct Signatures, tables of Chords in Positions and Inversions, exactly like the above. Give the name of each Chord and indicate Positions and Inversions, just as in our example.

E Minor:

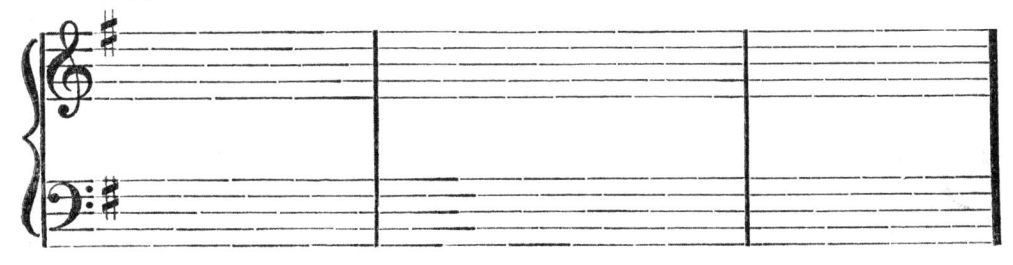

(Look out for Major Third).

B Minor:

(Student supply Signature).

HARMONY IN THE MINOR

(**Look** out for Major Third).

F♯ Minor:

C# Minor:

HARMONY IN THE MINOR

G♯ Minor:

E♭ Minor:

Bb Minor:

HARMONY IN THE MINOR

F Minor:

C Minor:

G Minor:

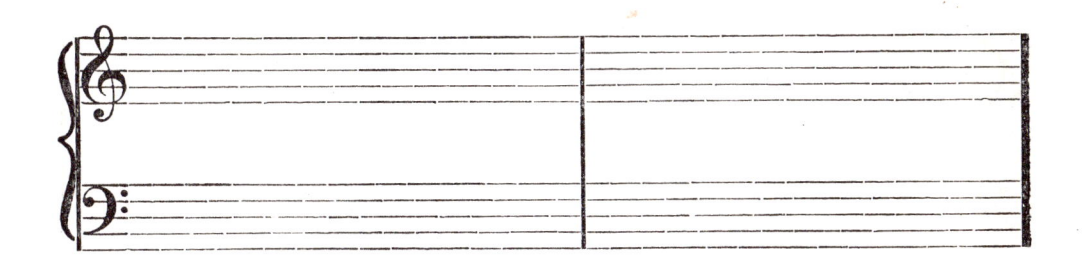

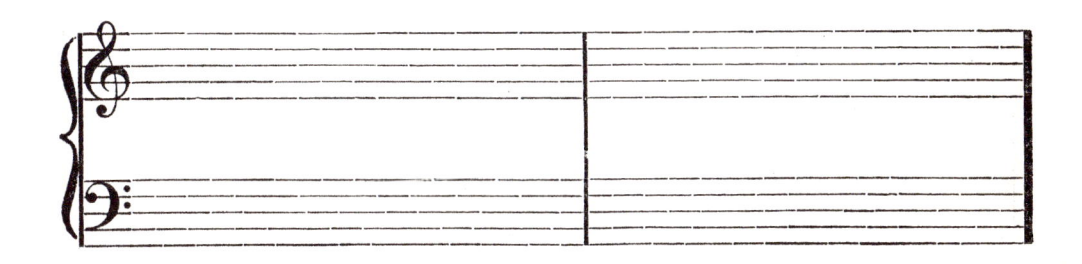

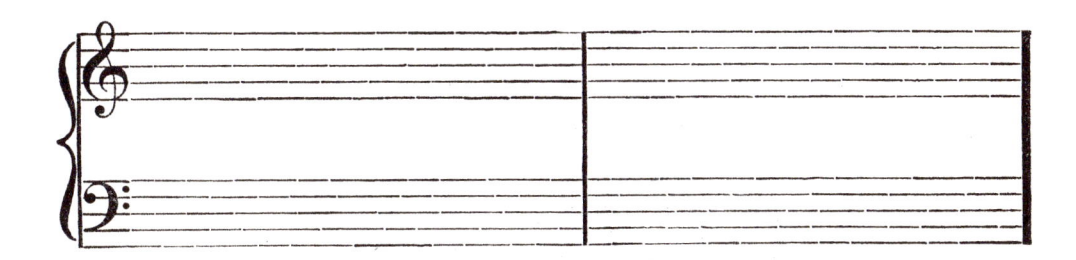

D Minor:

This is good practice.   Do not shirk it.

QUESTIONS

1. Which Triads to be found in the Harmonic Minor Scale contain Minor Thirds?
2. Which Triads contain Major Thirds?
3. Which Triads contain Perfect Fifths?
4. Which Triads contain Diminished Fifths?
5. Which Triad contains an Augmented Fifth?
6. How many Common Chords are available in the Harmonic Minor Scale?
7. Which of these Common Chords are Minor and which are Major?

CHAPTER XXI

HARMONY IN THE MINOR CONTINUED

Bearing in mind all the working principles so far attained, the student is now ready to harmonize some exercises in the Minor Scale.

The student will have noted that there is a skip of an **Augmented Second** from the *Sixth Degree* to the *Seventh Degree* of the **Harmonic Minor Scale**, thus: It is well to avoid this skip both in the Melody and in the Bass. Try to sing it at sight.

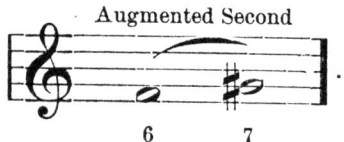

Here is a sample exercise completely analyzed:

1. The Tonic Chord, Third Position. Since the Signature is the *same*, both for the Major Scale and for its Relative Minor, the Tonic Chord (A Minor, in this case) tells us the Scale in which we are working.

2. The Submediant Chord, Fifth Position.

3. The Sub-Dominant Chord, Root Position.

4. The Dominant Chord, Fifth Position. This Chord also aids in settling the Scale in which we are working, since it contains (as its Third) the *chromatically raised Seventh Degree* or *Leading Note*. The **Leading Note** is very easy to harmonize, since it may *always* be treated as the **Third of the Dominant Chord.**

5. Tonic Chord, First Inversion (Fifth of the Chord doubled).

6. The Sub-Dominant Chord, Root Position.

7. The Tonic Chord, Second Inversion. This paves the way for the *Perfect Cadence* which follows (Chords 8 and 9).

8. The Dominant Chord, Fifth Position.

9. The Tonic Chord, Root Position.

Play and sing this Exercise. Note how smooth it is, how easily the Bass moves.

The above Analysis must be studied out, slowly and carefully, chord by chord. It tells some facts of the utmost importance.

Let the student write out an analysis of the next exercise, in the space provided below it. Give the Name of each Chord, its Position or Inversion. To begin with, tell in what Scale it is written.

90 OREM'S HARMONY BOOK

Scale of ?

1.
2.
3.
4.
5.
6.
7.
8.
9.
10.
11.
12.
13.
14.
15.
16.
17.

HARMONY IN THE MINOR CONTINUED

Here are some Basses for the student to harmonize. Notes not marked are, as usual, Roots of Chords; notes marked × are Thirds of Chords, requiring a First Inversion; notes marked ⦻ are Fifths of Chords, requiring a Second Inversion. See that *every Dominant Chord* has a *Major Third* (the Leading Note of the Scale).

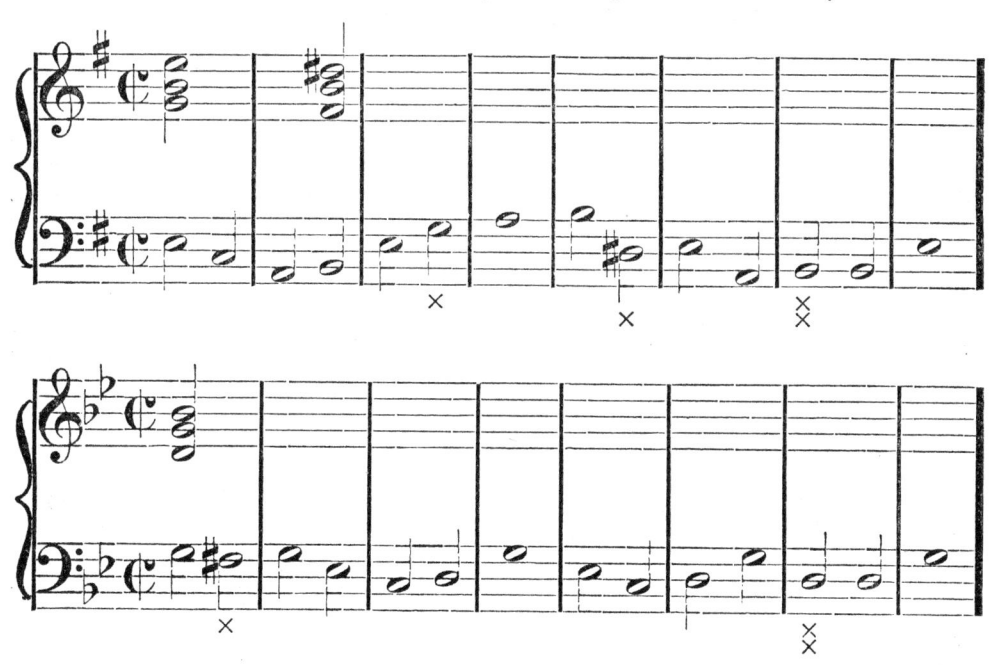

In the following Basses let the student pick out his own First and Second Inversions. Look out for the *Leading Note*. These will require study.

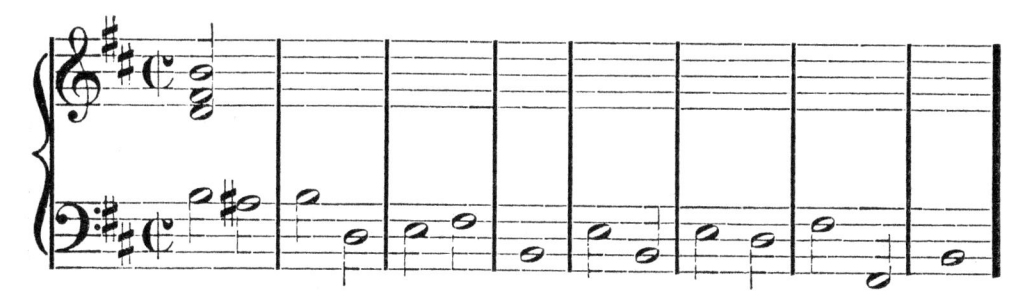

When a Bass note is found which can not be the Root of a Chord, it must be either a Third or a Fifth; but, more often than not, it is a Third, indicating a First Inversion. By this time the student knows where to look for a Second Inversion.

Here are some Melodies in the Minor which should not puzzle the student greatly if the preceding work has been well done. Bear in mind all past principles and precepts.

Use only such chords as are found in the Harmonic Minor Scale in which you are working.

HARMONY IN THE MINOR CONTINUED

QUESTIONS

1. What Interval is to be found between the Sixth and Seventh Degrees of the Harmonic Minor Scale?

2. What have you to say of this Interval?

3. What Chords serve to determine whether one is working in a Major Scale or in its Relative Minor?

4. What is the easiest note to harmonize, and how may it always be treated?

5. What kind of a Third must every Dominant Chord have?

6. What have you to say of a Bass note that can not be treated as the Root of a Chord?

CHAPTER XXII

THE FIGURED BASS

Thorough Bass, or **General Bass**, or **Figured Bass** is a sort of musical shorthand, in which, by the use of certain numerals and figures, singly and in combination, one may indicate the various Chords, their Positions and Inversions. It has always been used in the study and teaching of Harmony, although some works employ it sparingly, and others, nowadays, practically discard it. We will use it, in this book, from now on. It will have no terrors for the student who has mastered the preceding portion. It is a common means of ready reference among musicians.

To begin with, the Roots of Common Chords are indicated by **Roman Numerals**, corresponding to the various Degrees of the Scale. For Roots of *Major Chords large Numerals* are used; for Roots of *Minor Chords small Numerals* are used. In C Major, for instance, it would be thus:

I   II   III   IV   V   VI

In the case of the Chord on the Leading Note, or Diminished Triad, having a Diminished Fifth, a small Numeral with a cipher to the right is used, thus:

VII°

There are two Diminished Triads occurring in the Harmonic Minor Scale which are indicated similarly. In A Minor they would be thus:

II°   VII°

There is also on the Third Degree of the Harmonic Minor Scale an Augmented Triad (having a Major Third and Augmented Fifth). This is usually indicated by a large Roman Numeral with an accent to the right. In A Minor it would be thus:

III′

To sum up, the Triads in C Major would be indicated thus:

I   II   III   IV   V   VI   VII°

THE FIGURED BASS

The Triads in A Minor would be indicated thus:

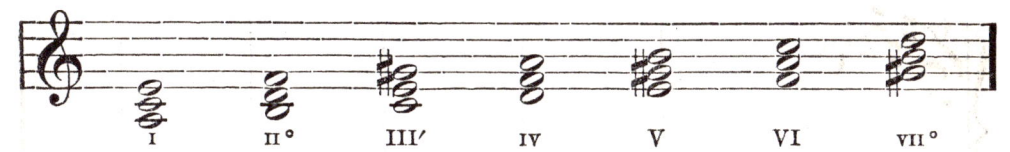

[musical notation: I, II°, III′, IV, V, VI, VII°]

These are not at all difficult to memorize, but it should be done at once.

Here are some exercises for the student, which will afford practice in the Numerals and, at the same time, serve as a review in Common Chords.

Each Bass Note is the *Root of a Chord*. Beneath each of these notes let the student write the appropriate Roman Numeral, also, indicate the Scales. Next, go ahead and harmonize as usual.

SCALE OF (?)

SCALE OF (?)

SCALE OF (?)

SCALE OF (?)

SCALE OF (?)

SCALE OF (?)

SCALE OF (?)

Here is some good practice in the Diminished and Augmented Triads. Under each of the following Triads, Scale and Signature given, let the student write the correct Roman Numeral, with its ° or ', as the case may be.

C Major   A Minor   G Major   E Minor

F Major   D Minor   D Major   B Minor

B♭ Major   G Minor   A Major   F♯ Minor

THE FIGURED BASS

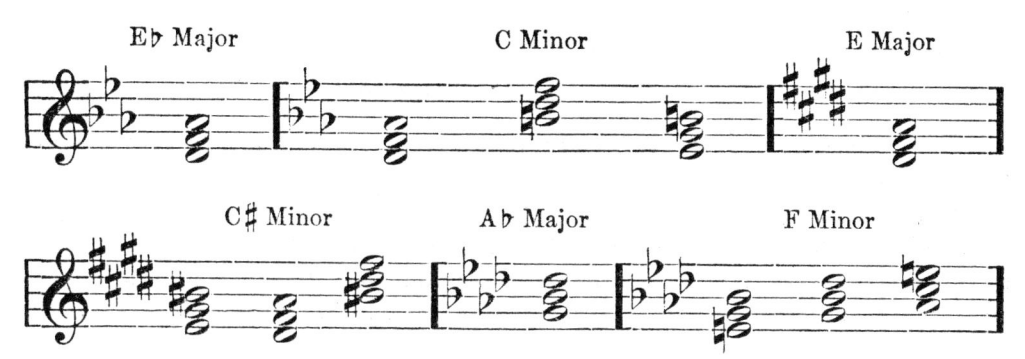

Eb Major **C Minor** **E Major**

C# Minor **Ab Major** **F Minor**

Now, in the following, according to the Scale, Signature and the Roman Numerals given, let the student write out the correct Diminished or Augmented Triads.

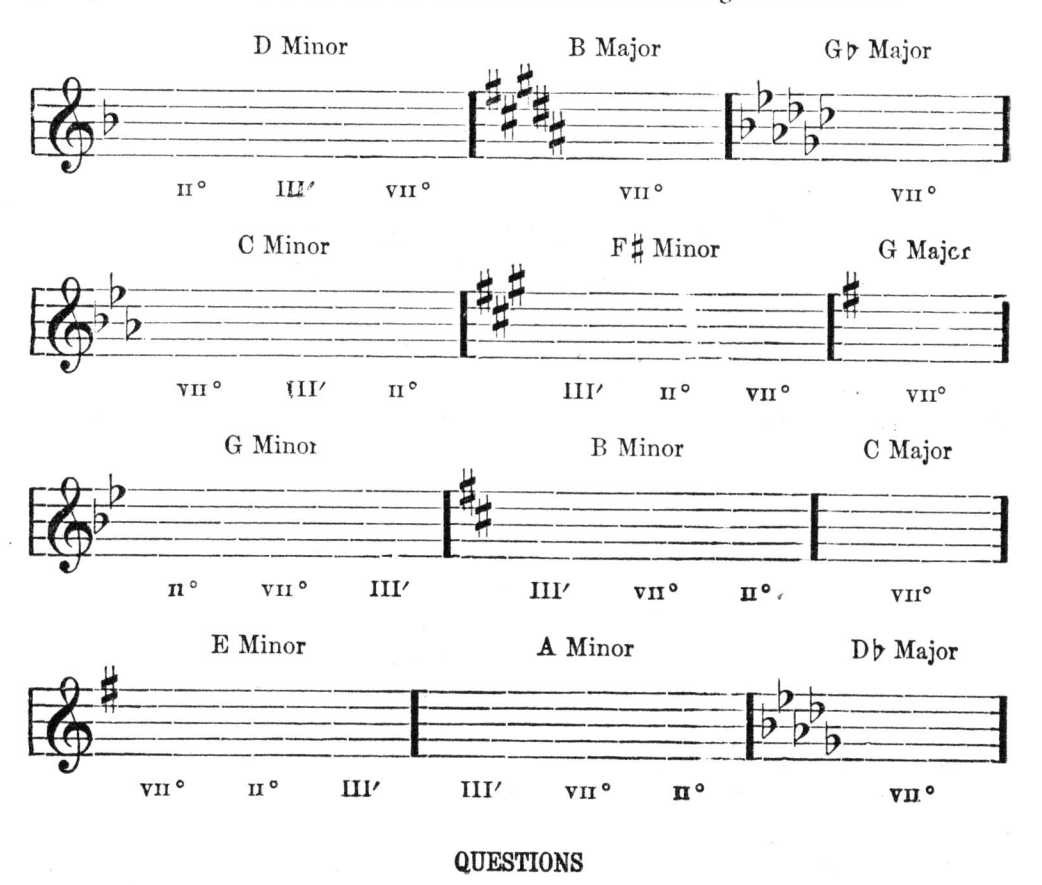

D Minor **B Major** **Gb Major**

II° III′ VII°   VII°   VII°

C Minor **F# Minor** **G Major**

VII° III′ II°   III′ II° VII°   VII°

G Minor **B Minor** **C Major**

II° VII° III′   III′ VII° II°   VII°

E Minor **A Minor** **Db Major**

VII° II° III′   III′ VII° II°   VII°

QUESTIONS

1. What is meant by Figured Bass?
2. By what other names is it known?
3. How do we indicate Major and Minor Triads according to this system?
4. How do we indicate Diminished Triads?
5. How do we indicate Augmented Triads?

CHAPTER XXIII

FIGURED BASS CONTINUED

In the preceding chapter we discussed the use of Roman Numerals. Now, as to the Figures.

When a Bass Note is written *without* Figures or *with* a Roman Numeral it is understood to be the Root of a Common Chord. Ordinarily the Position of the Chord is left to the student. Should it be necessary, however, to indicate the Position, this may be done by a Figure 8, 3, or 5, as the case may be, written immediately over the Bass Note. For instance, the following Bass:

would be written out:

All very simple. The Figures 8, 3, 5 *always* refer to *Positions*.

The Inversions are indicated plainly and clearly by means of Figures. Hereafter, when we have to refer to the *First Inversion* we will use a Figure 6. For instance:

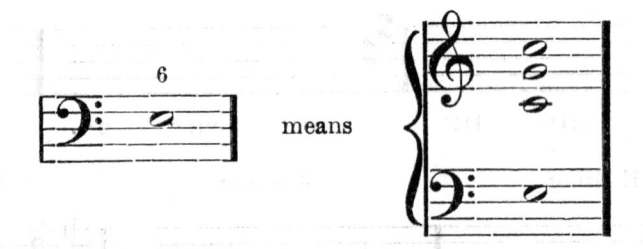

means

The reason for using the Figure 6 is, that, if we count up a *Sixth* from the given Bass note, we will obtain the *Root* of the Chord; the Bass Note, of course, being the Third of the Chord.

The **First Inversion** is commonly spoken of as the **Six Chord or Chord of the Sixth.**

Hereafter we will use the Figures $^6_4$ for the Second Inversion. For instance:

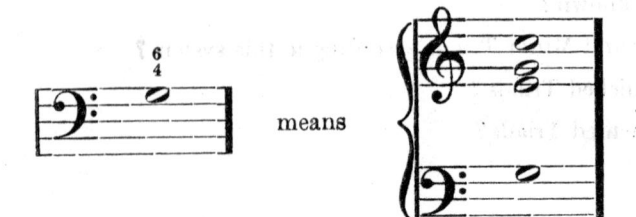

means

If we count up a *Fourth* from the

given Bass Note, we will obtain the *Root* of the Chord, the Bass Note, of course, being the Fifth of the Chord. Counting up a Sixth in the same manner we obtain the Third of the Chord.

The **Second Inversion** is commonly spoken of as the **Six-Four Chord** or **Chord of the Six-Four.**

Below is a Bass, figured in accordance with the preceding explanations. The student who has mastered the contents of this book, up to this point, should find it very easy to harmonize. Some may be able to play it at sight. All should try.

Here is the Bass:

And here is the Harmony:

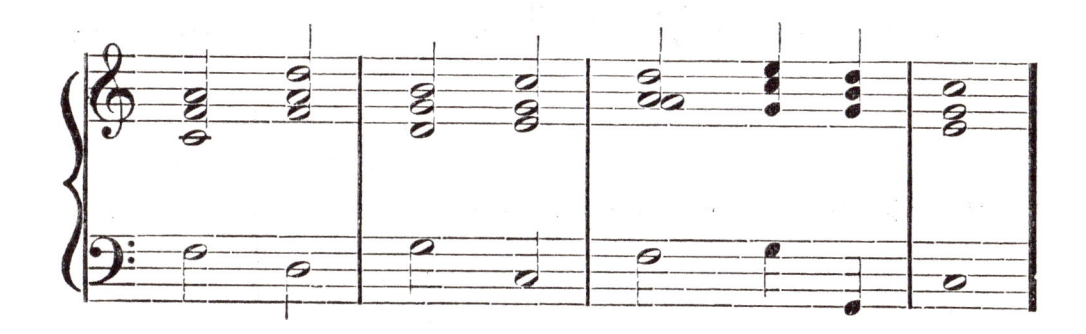

Now let the student try a few. See how quickly he can work them out. Remember all principles.

OREM'S HARMONY BOOK

Write the proper Roman Numeral under each chord, indicating its Root.

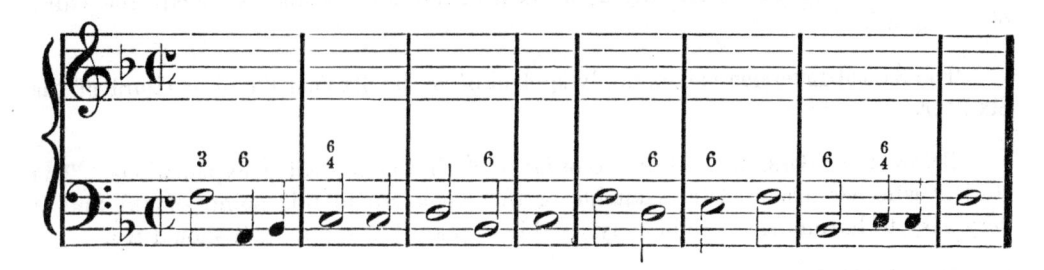

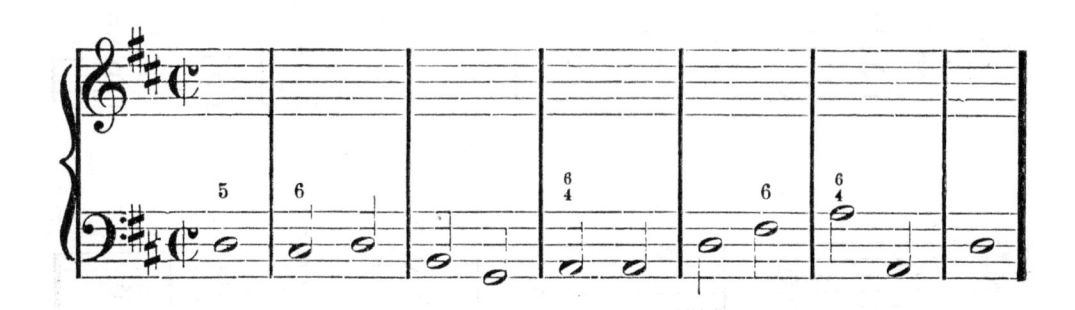

When a ♯, ♮ or 𝄪, as the case may be, with no Figure by its side, stands over a Bass Note, it shows that the same sign should be written before the Third over said Bass Note. For instance:  means that G, the Third over E, must be written G♯. The Chord will be completed thus:  This device is of special use in reminding us that the Leading Note in the Harmonic Minor Scale is always a chromatically raised note, being also the Major Third in the Dominant Chord.

FIGURED BASS CONTINUED

Bearing the preceding statement in mind let us now harmonize some Figured Basses in the various Minor Scales.

Here is an example:

Let us harmonize this Bass, writing also the proper Roman Numeral for the Bass Note of each Chord. Here it is. Analyze it carefully.

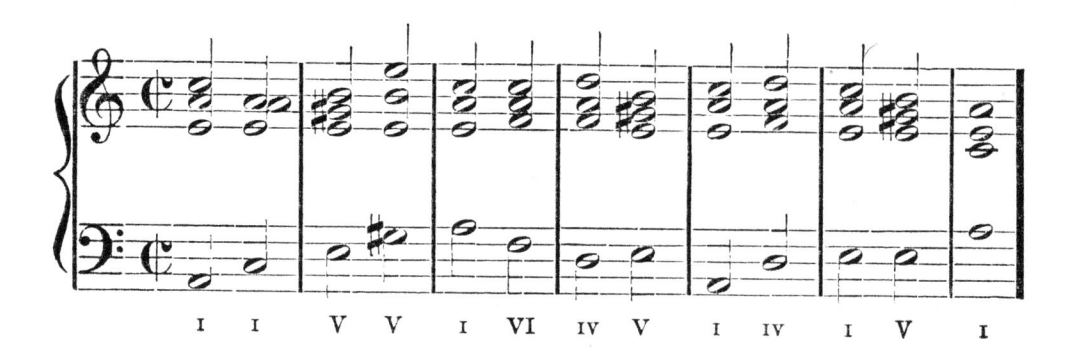

I I   V V   I VI   IV V   I IV   I V   I

Now let the student harmonize the following, in similar manner.

QUESTIONS

1. When a Bass Note is written *without* Figures or *with* a Roman Numeral what is it understood to be?

2. How is the Position of a Chord indicated?

3. How is a *First Inversion* indicated? Explain.

4. How is a *Second Inversion* indicated? Explain.

5. By what term do we commonly distinguish the *First Inversion?*

6. By what term do we commonly distinguish the *Second Inversion?*

7. What does a ♯, a ♮, or a ✕ written over a Bass Note mean? Give examples.

CHAPTER XXIV
MELODIES AND FIGURES

To prepare for harmonizing given Melodies with Figures, and in review of the foregoing chapters, let the student supply the proper Roman Numerals and Figures, where needed, in each of the following exercises. Write beneath each chord the Roman Numeral corresponding to the Root of the Chord. Indicate with the Figure 6 each First Inversion. Indicate with the Figures $^6_4$ each Second Inversion. Supply the necessary sign for a chromatically raised Third of a Chord. Indicate at the beginning of each exercise the Scale in which it is written. This is real Harmonic Analysis. Always try to imagine the effect of each chord. Afterwards play each exercise through slowly and see how nearly you were right.

SCALE OF (?)

In the following Melodies, the Scale is indicated at the beginning, followed by a series of Roman Numerals, each Numeral indicating the Root of the Chord to be used.

The Figures 6 and $\frac{6}{4}$ indicate the First and Second Inversions, respectively.

The Student must decide, first of all, upon the proper Bass Note to be used; then, write the Bass Note, and fill in the remainder of the Chord. This is fine practice.

Again, try to imagine how each exercise sounds, before playing it over.

Remember all the principles and suggestions of the foregoing chapters. All will be needed in working out these exercises smoothly. Be careful of the motion of the Bass part.

B♭: I I6 VI II6 I$^6_4$ V I VI II6 V I

V III VI IV V I6 IV II I$^6_4$ V I

A: I V6 I I6 V V6 I6 II VI6 VI V

MELODIES AND FIGURES

I_6 IV II V_6 | I I_6 | IV II I_4^6 V | I

E (Minor): I I_6 I_4^6 V♯ | I I_6 | IV$_6$ IV V♯ V$_6$♯ | I

I I_6 I_4^6 V♯ | I VI | IV IV$_6$ I_4^6 V♯ | I

E♭: I I_6 IV | I IV$_6$ I_4^6 V | I IV | V

I I_6 IV | I_4^6 V VI IV | I_4^6 V | I

No questions for this Chapter.

CHAPTER XXV

FREER USE OF CHORDS AND INVERSIONS

So far we have withheld from the student the prohibition found in all harmony books: **avoid parallel or consecutive fifths or octaves between any two parts or voices.** Modern composers pay little, if any, attention to this prohibition, so far as free instrumental writing is concerned; but in pure four part harmony, especially for practice, it should be strictly obeyed: Up to this point, by sticking to the principle that *no two Chords be written in succession in the same Position*, the student has avoided the bugbear of *consecutive Fifths and Octaves*. Let us illustrate:

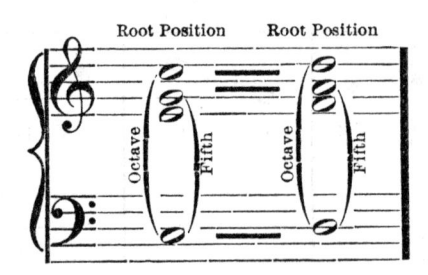

Here are Consecutive Octaves between the upper and lower parts in these two Chords: C-C and D-D; also, Consecutive Fifths between the Bass part and the next to the upper part: C-G and D-A. By writing the Chords in different Positions these would be avoided. Here is another example:

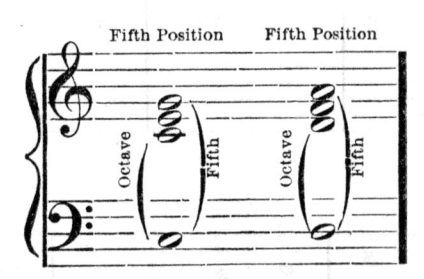

The remedy is the same. Change the Position of one of the Chords.

As two Octave Positions in succession, or two Fifth Positions in succession are rarely satisfactory, the student will not wish to use them anyway.

It is convenient at times to write two Third Positions in succession. If the **Third** of one of these Chords be **doubled** *instead of the Root*, Consecutive Fifths and Octaves will be avoided. This is not so difficult as it sounds. Let us illustrate:

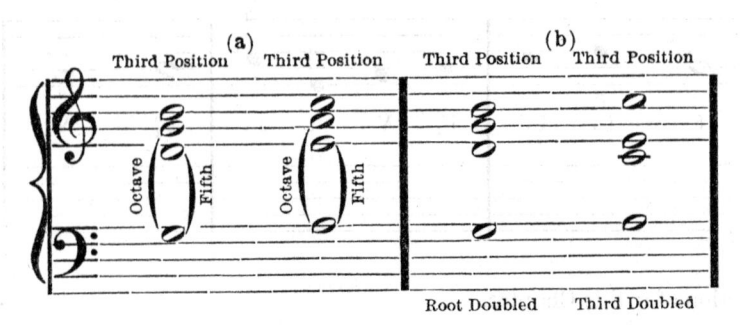

FREER USE OF CHORDS AND INVERSIONS

In the first two Chords, (a), each in the Third Position, with Root doubled, we find Consecutive Fifths and Octaves. In the same two Chords (b), each in the Third Position, but with the Third (C) of the second Chord doubled, instead of the Root (A), we find *no* Consecutive Fifths or Octaves.

Here is another similar example. Let the student mark this up, and analyze for himself.

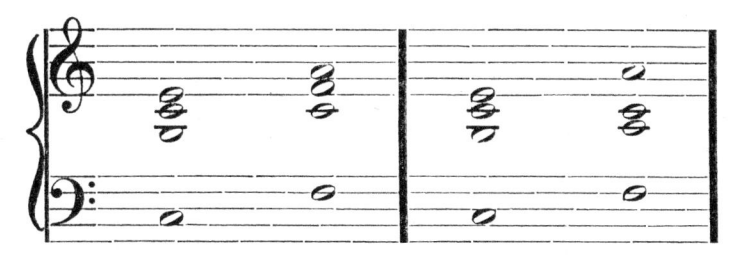

As we go on we shall have occasional use for this device.

This is the first time that we have doubled the Third of a Chord. In Positions we have doubled the Root only, and, in Inversions, the Fifth. In general, it is safe to say that the **Root of a Chord is the best to double; the Fifth is next best; the Third should be doubled but sparingly.**

So far we have not used the **Chord on the Leading Note** (vii° in the Scale). It is not satisfactory in the Positions but it sounds well in the **First Inversion**, *with its* **Third** *doubled*. Here is an effective way of bringing it in.

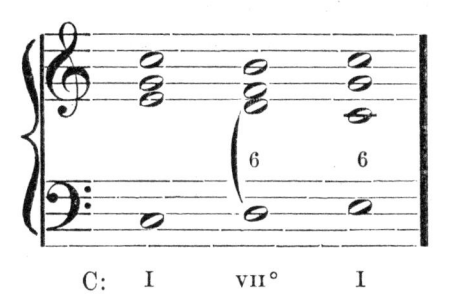

C: I   vii°   I

The second Chord is the Leading Note Chord, with its Third (D) doubled. Play this example and listen carefully.

The same Chord, occurring as the Supertonic (ii°) in the Minor Scale may also be used in the same manner, in the First Inversion, with its Third Doubled. Sometimes, in the *Minor Scale*, it is used with its *Root* in the Bass. Here is an example, showing both uses:

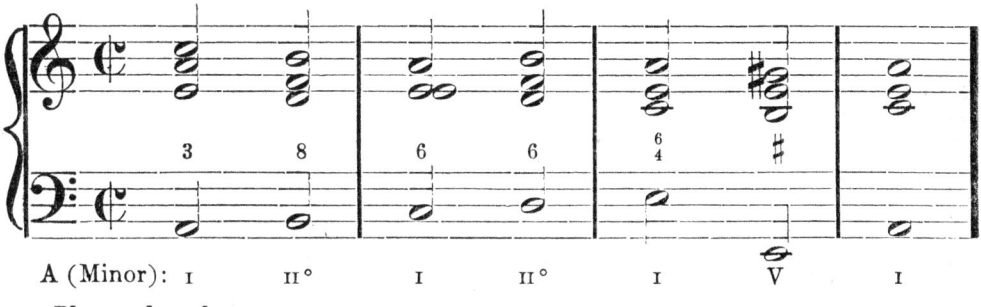

A (Minor): I   ii°   I   ii°   I   V   I

Play and analyze.

There is one more Chord in the Harmonic Minor Scale of which mention must be made: The Mediant Chord (III′). This Chord has a Major Third and *Augmented Fifth*. It may be used in the Positions or in the First Inversion. In the Positions, the *Root*, of course, should be doubled. In the First Inversion, the *Root* or *Third* may be doubled. Here are some examples:

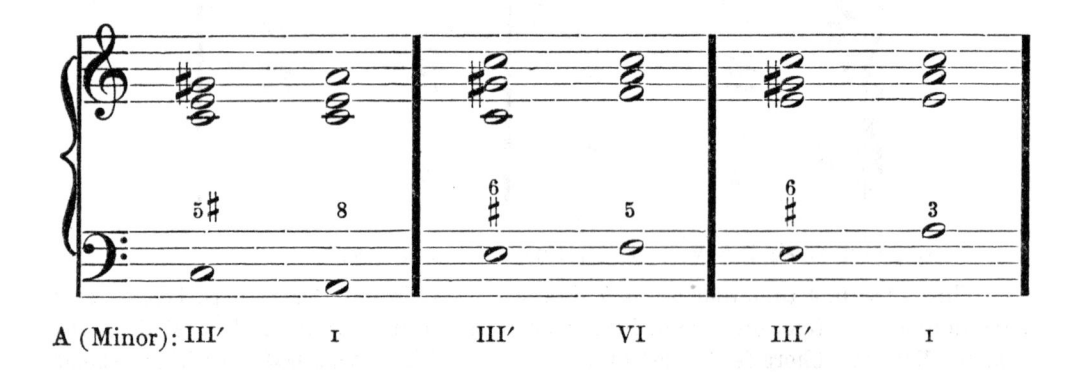

A (Minor): III′   I   III′   VI   III′   I

Now for some exercises introducing these additional harmonic resources. Bear in mind all principles and explanations.

First of all, some Figured Basses. Let the student supply the Roman Numerals and indicate the Scale. Look out, from now on, for *Consecutive Fifths or Octaves*.

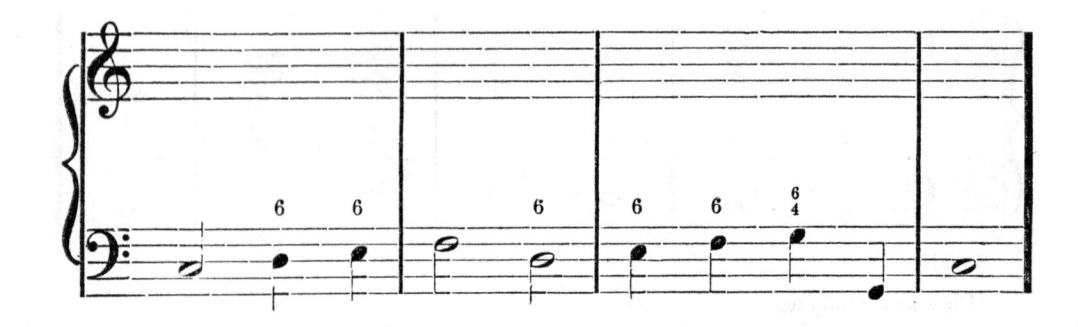

FREER USE OF CHORDS AND INVERSIONS

Although, by this time, the student should have the Figured Bass at his finger ends, it should not be relied upon entirely.

The student should apply all his knowledge in harmonizing the following exercises.

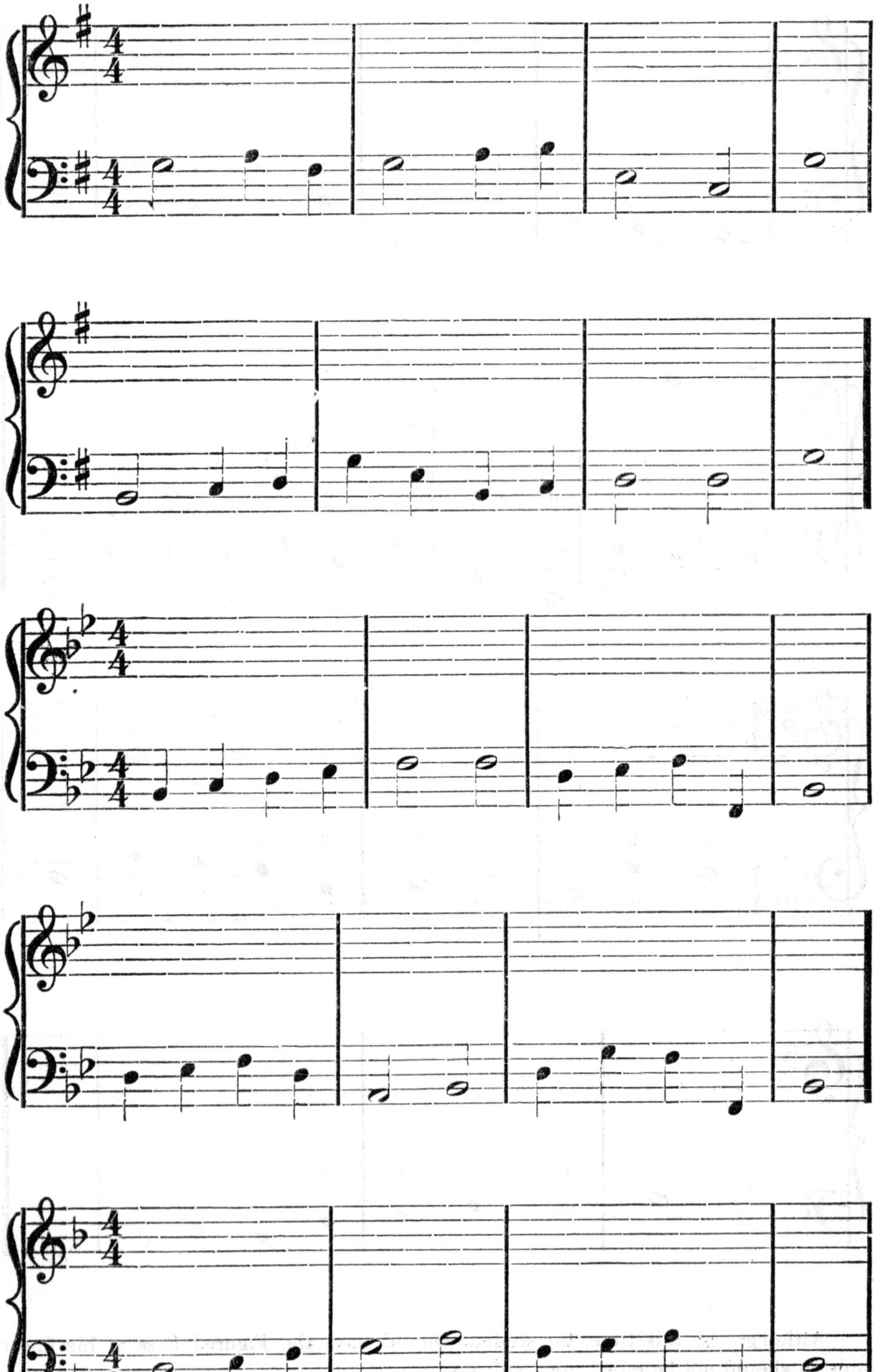

FREER USE OF CHORDS AND INVERSIONS

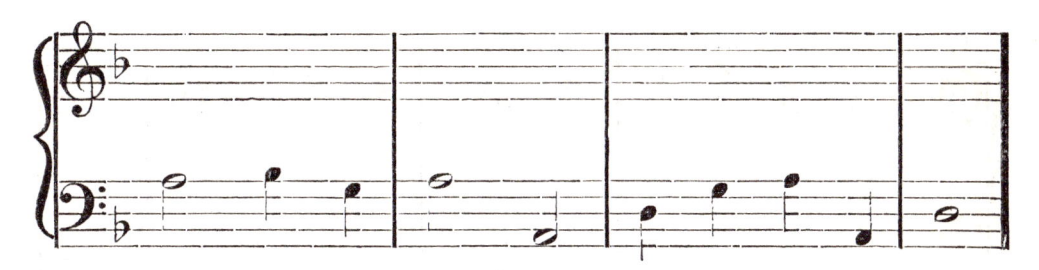

The foregoing *must be made* to sound well.

Now try some melodies.

QUESTIONS

1. What is the prohibition regarding Fifths and Octaves?

2. How may two Third Positions be written in succession?

3. What have you to say regarding the doubling of the Root, the Third, or the Fifth of any Chord?

4. How may the Chord of the Leading Note be used?

5. How may the Supertonic Chord of the Harmonic Minor Scale be used?

6. How may the Mediant Chord of the Harmonic Minor Scale be used?

CHAPTER XXVI
ADDITIONAL USES OF THE SECOND INVERSION

So far we have used the Second Inversion ($^6_4$) of the Tonic Chord only. We have done so to avoid confusion, especially in view of the fact that the Tonic is by far the most important Chord to use in this manner.

Other Chords in any Scale which may be used with good effect in the **Second Inversion** are the **Dominant** and **Subdominant Chords**. All these $^6_4$ Chords require special attention, since they are *never* satisfactory if allowed to stand alone. That is to say, they sound best when followed by certain other Chords, and, in some cases, when preceded by others. Young composers, and, for that matter, many who are old enough to know better frequently fail in the use of the $^6_4$ Chord. By following the few brief directions here given, one can never go astray in this matter.

We have already discussed the use of the Tonic $^6_4$. The **Dominant** $^6_4$ sounds best when preceded by the *Third Position of the Tonic* and followed by the *First Inversion of the Tonic*, or the other way about. Analyze the following example and see how it is done. Play it too, and hear how smooth it is.

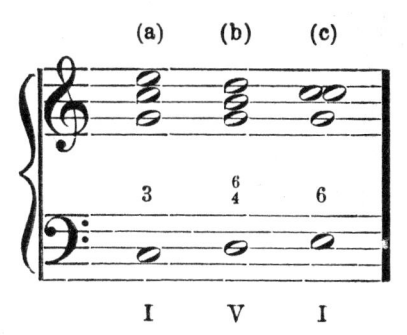

At (a) we have the Third Position of the Tonic Chord; at (b), the Second Inversion ($^6_4$) of the Dominant Chord; at (c), the First Inversion (6) of the Tonic Chord. Taking it the other way about, we would have it thus:

Note that both Melody and Bass in either example move Diatonically and in Contrary Motion. This is the best and simplest way of harmonizing such passages. It should be easily remembered.

The **Second Inversion** ($^6_4$) of the **Subdominant** sounds best when *preceded* and *followed* by the *Tonic* (Root in the Bass). Analyze the following example, play and listen.

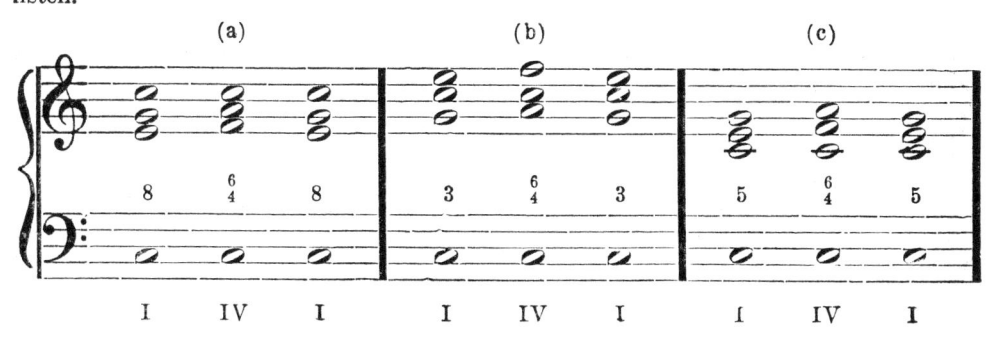

At (a) we have the Root Position of the Tonic Chord, followed by the Subdominant $^6_4$, followed by the Root Position of the Tonic. At (b) and (c) we have the same three Chords in other Positions. This is also easy to remember. Note that we have the same Bass Note three times in succession.

Here is a complete example introducing 6 and $^6_4$ Chords according to the foregoing precepts. Let the student analyze this example and write in carefully both the Roman Numerals and the Figured Bass before going further. Play the example, and sing it too.

After having mastered this example the student is ready for some Basses, introducing 6 and $^6_4$ Chords in their various uses. These must all be made to sound well. If properly done, they should prove very satisfactory. In these we give the Figures. Let the student add the Roman Numerals, also the name of the Scale.

ADDITIONAL USES OF THE SECOND INVERSION

The following, in the Minor, should sound well.

ADDITIONAL USES OF THE SECOND INVERSION

The following Basses are without Figures. Let the student apply the knowledge so far gained, and harmonize them smoothly, introducing 6 and $^6_4$ Chords, according to taste and opportunity. *Make* them sound well.

Finally, let the student harmonize these Melodies, using all the resources at his command. Do not leave any one of them until it sounds well, proving satisfactory in all respects.

ADDITIONAL USES OF THE SECOND INVERSION

QUESTIONS

1. Besides the Tonic, what other Chords may be used in the Second Inversion?
2. How should each of these Second Inversions be preceded and followed?

CHAPTER XXVII
THE DOMINANT SEVENTH CHORD

The **Seventh** may be added to the **Dominant Chord.** As an example, take G–B–D, the Dominant Chord in C Major, and add to it F (the *Seventh*), thus:

Scale of C — Seventh, Fifth, Third, Root
The Dominant Chord with Seventh added.

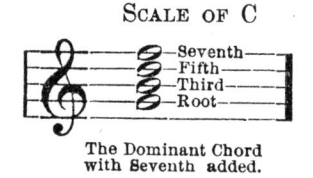

Up to this point we have been working with Triads, or Three-Tone Chords, in which we had to double a Member in order to give a Four-Part Harmony, but the addition of the Seventh to the Dominant Chord gives us a complete *Four-Tone Chord.* It is known as the **Dominant Seventh Chord.** This Chord is one of the most important, and most used, Chords in all Music. It lies at the very foundation of all so-called **Dissonant Harmony.**

By a **Dissonant Interval** we mean one which does not appear to be satisfactory standing by itself, but which appears to lean upon some other Interval. Take this very Interval about which we have been talking: the *Seventh* (a Minor Seventh, by the way). Strike it by itself, and listen: . It seems to need something to follow. Now strike it again, and allow the *Seventh* (F) to *descend One Degree* (to E or E♭) and the ear is satisfied, thus: . This motion of a *Dissonant Member* of a Chord is called its **Resolution.** **Consonant Intervals,** Thirds, Fifths, Sixths and Octaves, such as we have been using up to this point, are satisfactory in themselves and do not require Resolution.

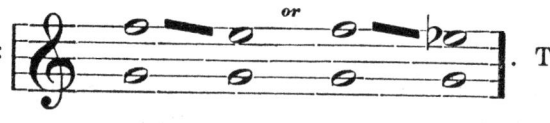

Since the Seventh requires Resolution, it stands to reason that whichever Chord follows the Dominant Seventh Chord must contain that Tone upon which the Seventh resolves. In our example we found F (the Seventh) resolving upon E or E♭. Now we know E to be the Third of the Tonic Chord of C Major (C–E–G), and E♭ to be the Third of the Tonic Chord of C Minor. We also know, from our study of the Cadences that the Tonic is the most likely Chord with which to follow the Dominant. Let us see how the several parts or voices will move.

We know already that the *Seventh* is to descend: . 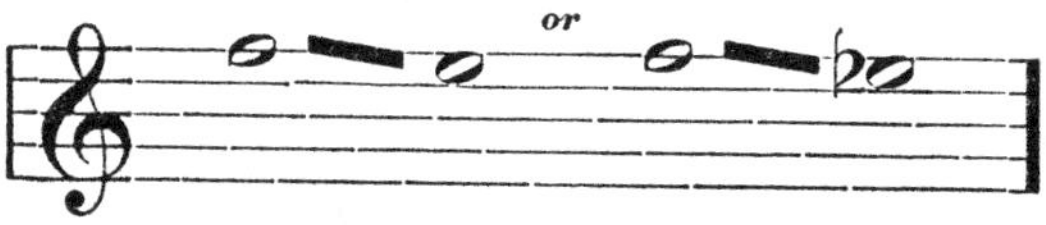
Seventh Descending

The *Third* of the Dominant Seventh Chord, being the *Leading Note* in the Scale always has an upward tendency: . This leaves the Fifth of the Chord
Leading Note Ascending

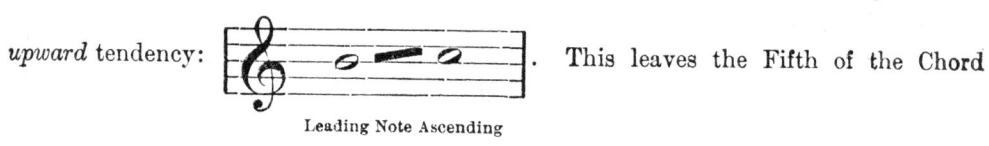

free to *ascend* or *descend*, but it *frequently descends*:

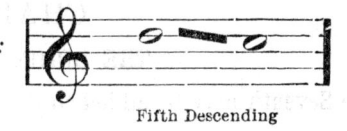

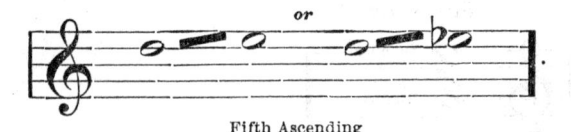

Fifth Descending

Fifth Ascending

. When the Root is in the Bass, it *ascends a Fourth* or *descends a Fifth*:

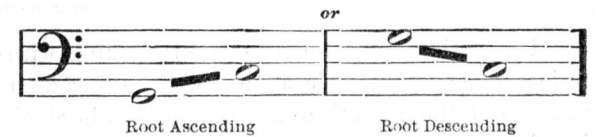

Root Ascending   Root Descending

Finally, the whole Dominant Seventh Chord will move towards the Tonic Chord in this manner:

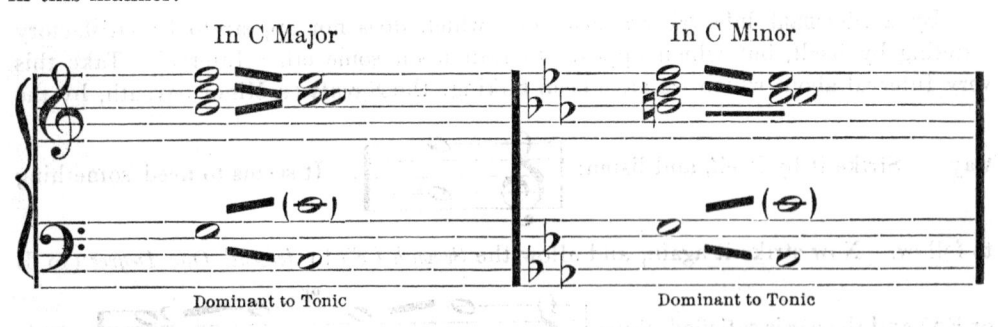

In C Major   In C Minor

Dominant to Tonic   Dominant to Tonic

It will be observed that, in the Tonic Chord, the *Fifth* of the Chord (G) *is absent*. The reason is obvious: there is no Member to lead to it. **The Fifth of any Common Chord may be omitted at any time.**

This leading of the Dominant Seventh Chord towards the Tonic Chord is known as a **Progression**.

Here is a chance for some fine ear training. The student will hear this Progression about as often as he will hear anything in Music. Let him learn to recognize it at once.

It will have been noted that *all Chords are built up in Thirds.* Consequently, the adding of the Seventh is but another step in the ladder. So far we have had Root, Third, Fifth (each a Third apart); now we have the Seventh in addition. All Chords are built up in this manner.

The Dominant Seventh Chord, with its *Root in the Bass*, may be written in three Positions, having its Seventh, its Fifth, or its Third at the top, thus:

Seventh   Fifth   Third

THE DOMINANT SEVENTH CHORD

Now for an exercise. We will write out the Dominant Seventh in C Major and C Minor, in its three Positions, following each Position by the appropriate Position of the Tonic Chord, according to the foregoing directions for the leading of the parts or voices. In a similar manner, let the student write out the same Progressions in the remaining Major and Minor Scales, in the spaces provided. Look out for the chromatically raised Thirds in Dominant Chords of the Minor Scales.

C Major: C Minor:

Let the student write in the Signatures according to the Scales indicated.

G Major: G Minor:

D Major: D Minor:

A Major: A Minor:

OREM'S HARMONY BOOK

E Major:

E Minor:

B Major.

B Minor:

Pay close attention to the Enharmonic changes following. Each of these pairs of Dominants is alike in sound, but the manner of writing differs.

G♭ Major:

F♯ Minor:

D♭ Major:

C♯ Minor:

A♭ Major:

G♯ Minor:

THE DOMINANT SEVENTH CHORD

E♭ Major: E♭ Minor:

B♭ Major: B♭ Minor:

F Major: F Minor:

The Dominant Seventh Chord with its Root in the Bass is Figured 7, thus: , the Position being left to the taste and judgment of the writer or player.

The Dominant Seventh Chord with its Root in the Bass is very effective following a Tonic $^6_4$ Chord; the Dominant Seventh Chord, in turn, being followed by the Tonic Chord (Root in the Bass). Thus:

I V I   I V I   I V I

Play these examples and learn to recognize them. They occur constantly in musical composition.

Here is a short example for the student to analyze. Write in both the Roman Numerals and the Figures.

Here are some Basses for the Student to work out. Dominant Sevenths with Roots in the Bass are introduced occasionally. Figures are given. Avoid *Consecutive Fifths and Octaves.*

QUESTIONS

1. What do you mean by the Dominant Seventh Chord?
2. What do you mean by a Dissonant Interval?
3. What do you mean by a Consonant Interval?
4. What do you mean by Resolution?
5. In following the Dominant Seventh Chord by the Tonic Chord, how do the various Members move.
6. What Member of a Common Chord may be omitted?
7. What do you mean by a Progression?
8. How are all Chords built up?
9. In how many Positions may the Dominant Seventh Chord, with Root in the Bass, be written? What are they?
10. How do you Figure the Dominant Seventh Chord, with Root in the Bass?

CHAPTER XXVIII
INVERSIONS OF THE DOMINANT SEVENTH CHORD

The Dominant Seventh Chord may be inverted at any time, and in any manner. By this we mean that any Member may be used in the Bass and any Member at the top. This will give us *Three Inversions* of the Dominant Seventh Chord, as follows:

Inversions of the Dominant Seventh Chord:

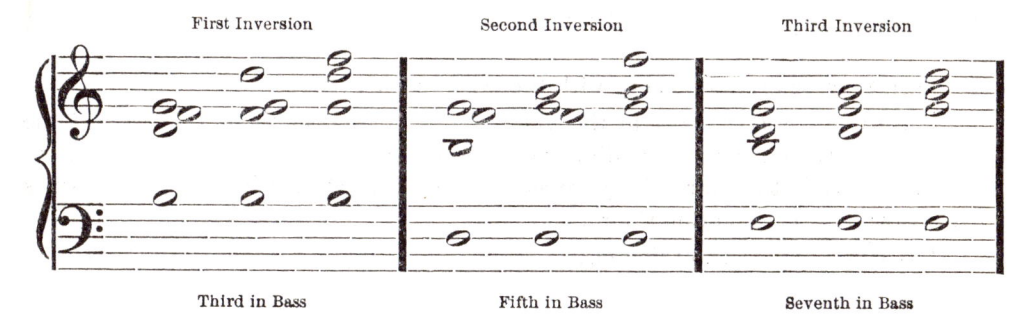

Play and sing all these, and make an ear test of them.

Now let the student write out in a similar manner the several Inversions of the Dominant Seventh Chords in the Scales given below.

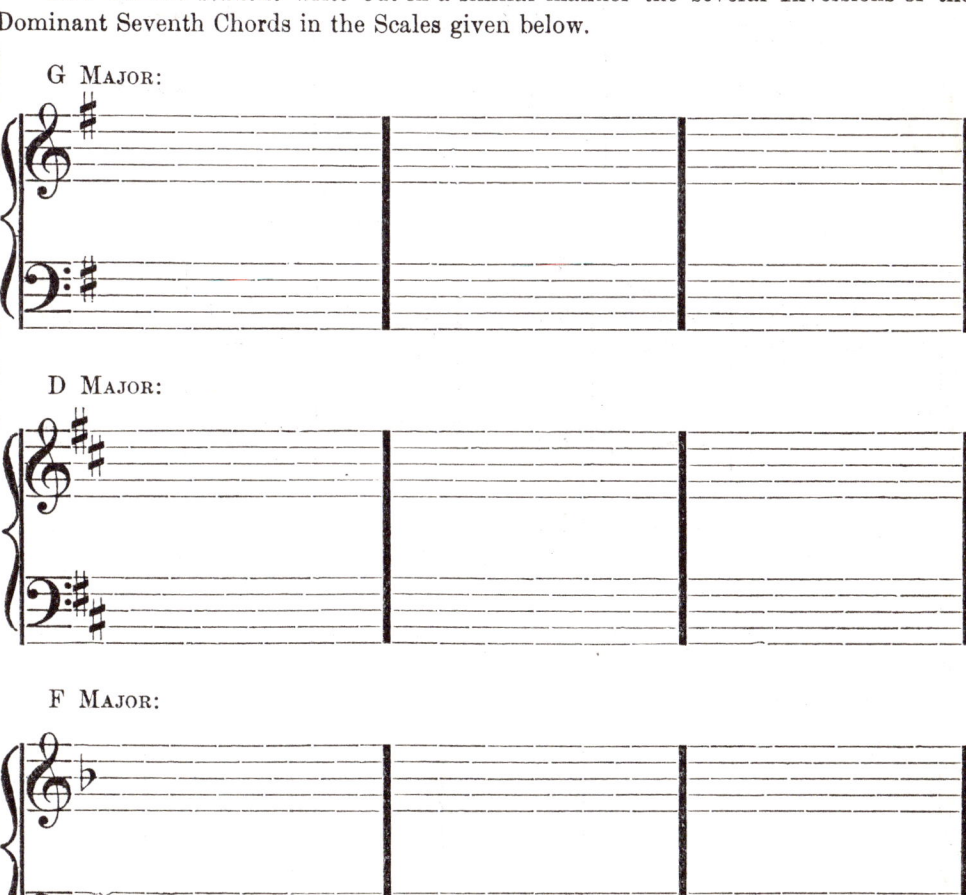

G Major:

D Major:

F Major:

B♭ Major:

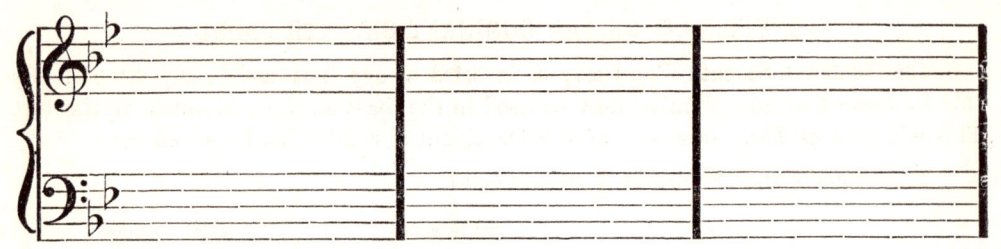

Learn to recognize these, both with the eye and the ear.

Now, as to the *Progression* to the *Tonic* Chord of each of these *Inversions* of the *Dominant Seventh Chord:* the Seventh always descends; the Fifth descends, preferably, but it may ascend; the Third always ascends; the Root, when it is *not* in the Bass, is carried over into the following Chord.

Here is the practical working out:

C Major:
    First Inversion.

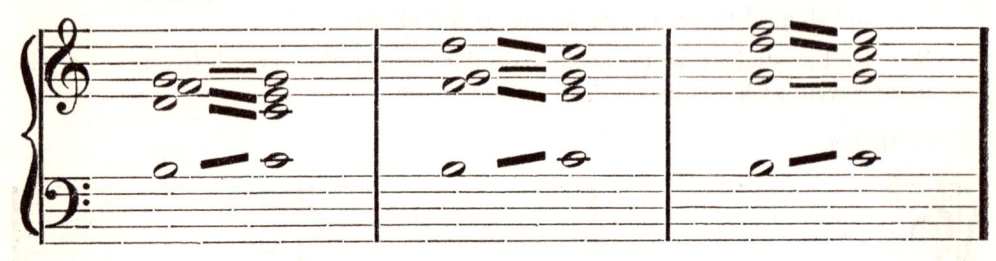

    Second Inversion.   Third Inversion.

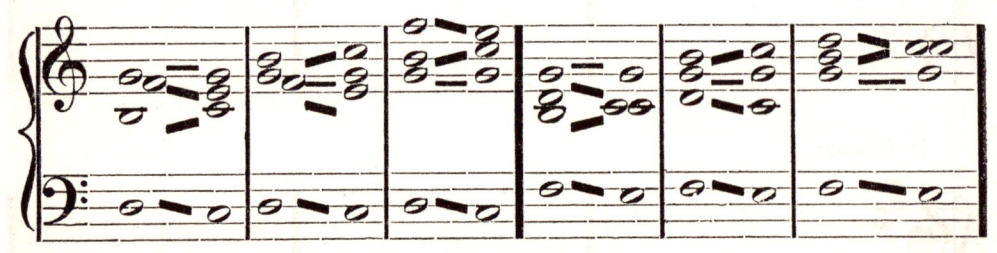

Note how beautifully each of these Inversions of the Dominant Seventh Chord leads into a Position or Inversion of the complete Tonic Chord. Make an eye and an ear test of this example.

Now let the student write out the foregoing example complete in each of the Scales specified.

G Major:

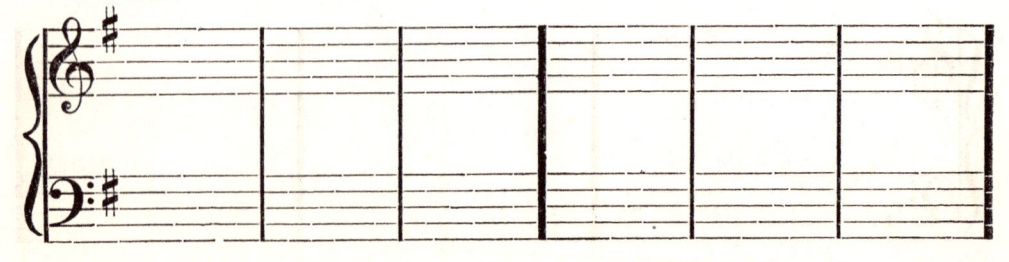

INVERSIONS OF THE DOMINANT SEVENTH CHORD

F Major:

D Major:

B♭ Major:

The foregoing will prove splendid practice. It will hardly be necessary to write these out in the Minor Scales at this time. The Progressions are identical, except for the fact that the Minor Tonic Chord must contain a Minor Third.

The following exercise will prove profitable and interesting. A number of Dominant Seventh Chords are given, in various Positions and Inversions. The student will write in the proper Major Tonic Chord after each Dominant, at the same time marking in the leading of the various Members of each Chord, just as in the foregoing examples. The first one is done complete, as a model for the following ones. It will be necessary for the student to analyze each Dominant Seventh Chord. Rearrange the notes of each one, mentally, so that the Chord will *read up in Thirds*. When you are sure of the *Root* of the Dominant Seventh Chord, it will be easy enough to locate the proper Tonic Chord.

The foregoing exercise must not be left until it is worked out correctly in every detail. Make an ear training exercise of it, also.

The Three Inversions of the Dominant Seventh Chord are Figured (with Roman Numerals) as follows:—

First Inversion: $\substack{6\\5}$ V_7 ; Second Inversion: $\substack{4\\3}$ V_7

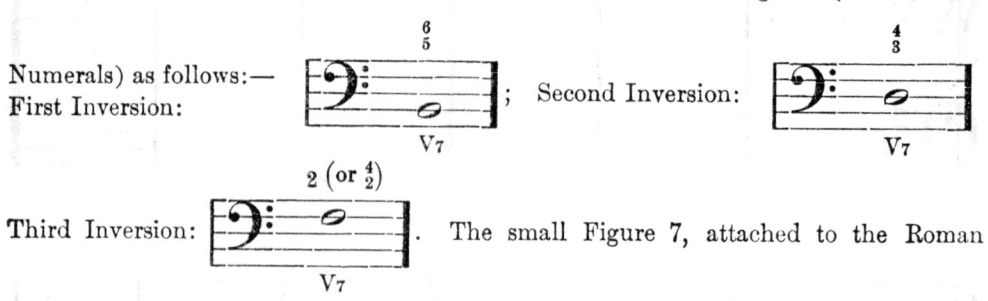

Third Inversion: $2 \text{ (or } \substack{4\\2})$ V_7 . The small Figure 7, attached to the Roman Numeral V, signifies Dominant Seventh Chord. After the student understands the Chord itself, there will be no trouble with the Figures. The various Positions are left to the taste and judgment of the student.

Now for an example introducing Positions and Inversions of the Dominant Seventh Chord. Figures and Numerals are given; but let the student analyze carefully. Play and sing many times.

INVERSIONS OF THE DOMINANT SEVENTH CHORD

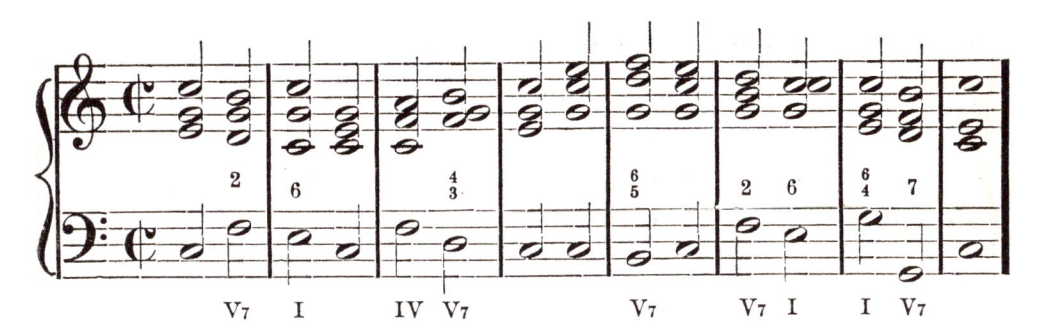

And here are some Basses for the student. Work them out slowly and carefully, applying every bit of the knowledge so far attained. This *must* sound well.

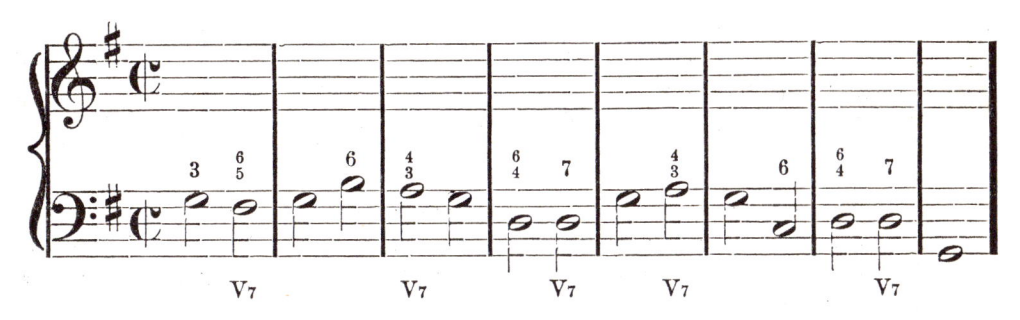

In the following, Roman Numerals may be added by the student. Figures only are given, and these only where necessary.

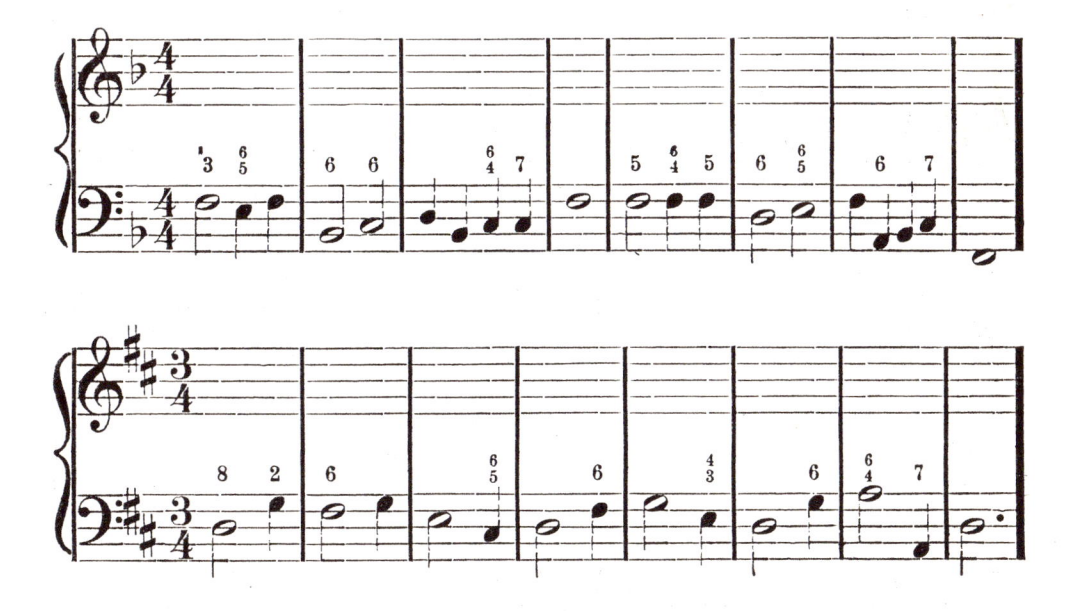

In Figuring the Second Inversion of the Dominant Seventh Chord in Minor Scales, the Chromatically raised Third of the Chord is indicated by a 6, in connection with the $\frac{4}{3}$, making it, as usually written, $\frac{6}{4}$, the *stroke* through any Figure requiring the indicated *member* to be *Chromatically raised*. In Figuring the Third Inversion it will be written $\frac{4}{2}$, for the same reason.

Let the student harmonize the following Basses and Melodies in his own way, according to experience, taste and judgment, introducing Dominant Seventh Chords, in Positions and Inversions, wherever they seem to be required. All the exercises must be made to sound well.

INVERSIONS OF THE DOMINANT SEVENTH CHORD

QUESTIONS

1. How may the Dominant Seventh Chord be inverted?

2. How many Inversions of the Dominant Seventh Chord are there? Describe them.

3. In the Progression of the Dominant Seventh Chord to the Tonic Chord, when an Inversion of the Dominant Seventh Chord is used, how do the various Members of this Chord move?

4. What is the best way to proceed in analyzing a Chord?

5. How are the Inversions of the Dominant Seventh Chord Figured?

6. In Figuring the Inversions of the Dominant Seventh Chord in the Minor Scale, how is the Chromatically raised Third of this Chord indicated?

CHAPTER XXIX
FURTHER USES OF THE DOMINANT SEVENTH CHORD — SEQUENCES

The Dominant Seventh Chord is sometimes used with its Fifth omitted, and with its Root Doubled. Occasionally this is both effective and convenient. When the Chord is used in this manner, the Root, if in the Bass, moves up a Fourth or down a Fifth. In any of the upper parts it is carried over.

Here are some examples:

The Dominant Seventh Chord, Fifth omitted, Root Doubled.

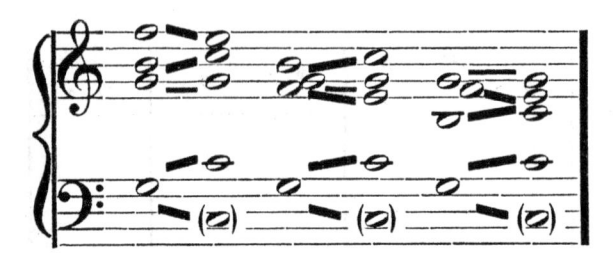

Let the student write out the foregoing example in each of the Scales specified below. Make an ear test of it also.

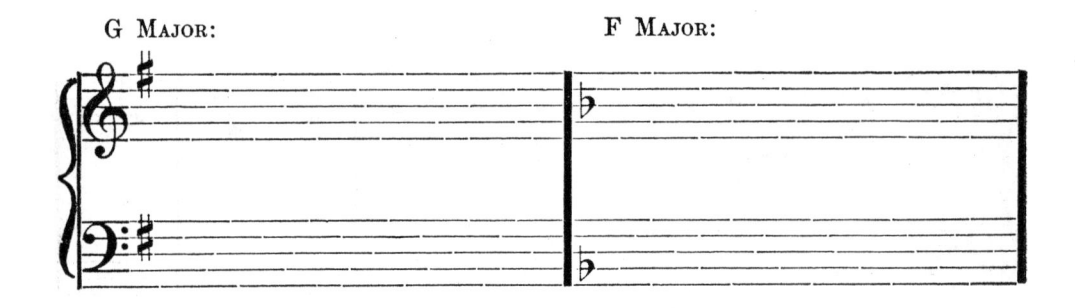

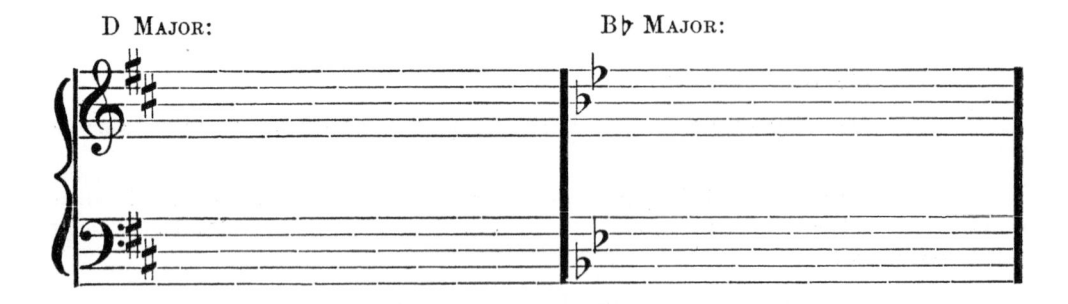

G Major:

F Major:

D Major:

B♭ Major:

The Dominant Seventh Chord may be used in the foregoing manner whenever desired.

Although the Progression from the Dominant Seventh Chord to the Tonic Chord is the most usual one, there are a number of other Progressions of the Dominant Seventh Chord to be found. The majority of these need not be considered in this book; but there is one useful Progression which should be taken up at this time.

The **Dominant Seventh Chord** may be followed by the **Submediant Chord.** In making this *Progression* the *Root of either Chord* should be found in the Bass. The various Members move, as follows: the Seventh descends; the Fifth descends; the Third ascends; the Root ascends (one Degree). Here is the way it is done:

FURTHER USES OF THE DOMINANT SEVENTH CHORD — SEQUENCES

Progression of the Dominant Seventh Chord to the Submediant Chord.

Here it is in the Minor Scale.

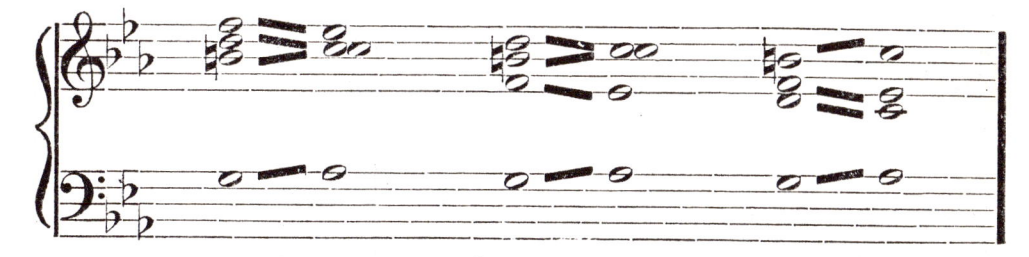

This Progression of the Dominant Seventh Chord is particularly useful in avoiding a Perfect Cadence. Continually following the Dominant Seventh Chord by the Tonic Chord seems like coming to too many full stops. The Progression to the Submediant seems to avoid a full stop, indicating something more to come. Prove this by playing and singing this Progression. Learn to recognize it when heard.

In the following example the Dominant Seventh Chord is introduced with its Fifth omitted and Root doubled. The Progression to the Submediant Chord is also introduced. Let the student make his own analysis of this example adding the appropriate Roman Numerals and Figures.

Here are some Basses and Melodies for the student. Work them out without any Figured Bass, using all the knowledge so far attained.

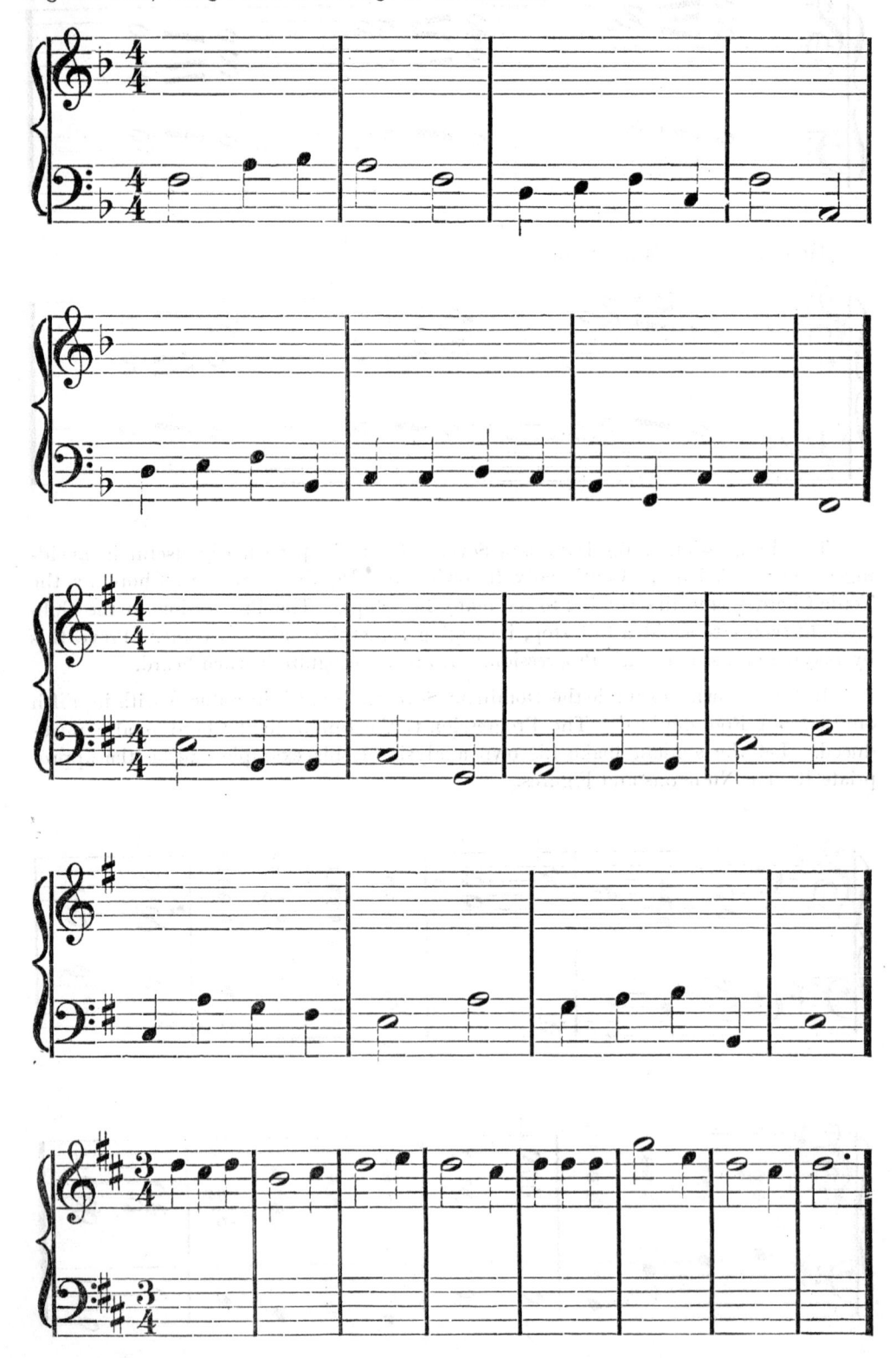

FURTHER USES OF THE DOMINANT SEVENTH CHORD — SEQUENCES

A Succession of a number of Chords moving according to some regular pattern or design is known as a Sequence. Here is an example which will illustrate the definition:

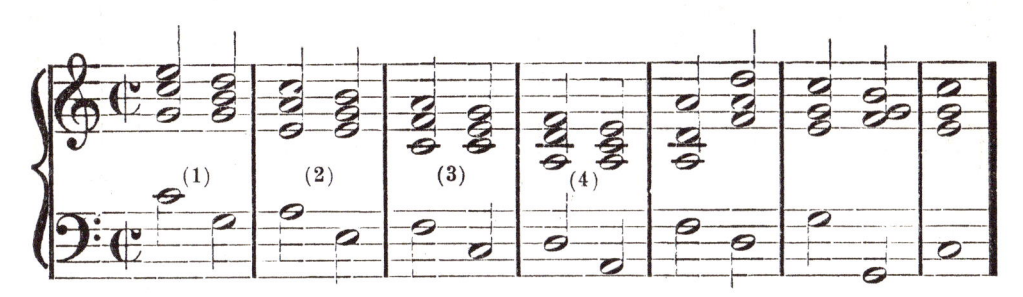

Play and sing this example.

At (1) we have a Chord in the Third Position followed by another Chord in the Fifth Position. At (2) we have the same thing, a Third lower. At (3) we have the same thing, a Third lower than at (2). At (4) we have the same thing, a Third lower than at (3). This forms a regular pattern. Moreover, take notice that the Bass notes form a pattern of their own, moving down a Fourth, up a Second, down a Fourth, up a Second, and so on. The Melody, also, moves right on down in Seconds. The remaining five Chords are used merely to complete the example musically.

Here is another example, containing a Sequence, in which a Third Position is followed by a First Inversion, and so on, and so on. In forming Sequences, Imperfect Chords are introduced freely, wherever needed; for instance, at (a):

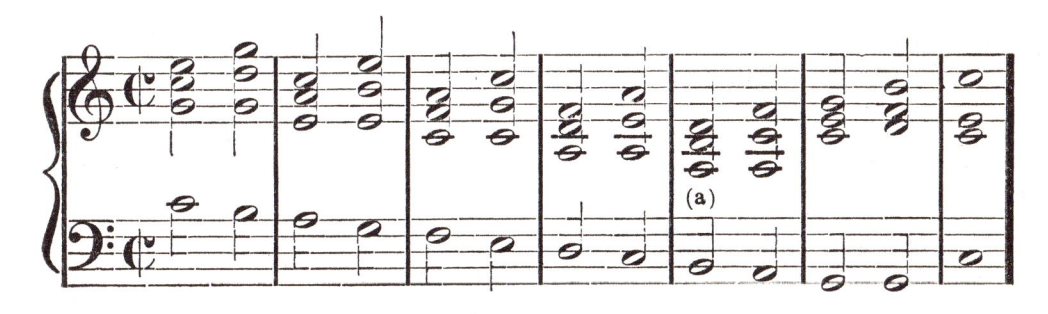

In forming Sequences a certain freedom of motion is allowable. The *pattern* is the most important thing.

In the following Basses the student will find opportunities for making Sequences, and for applying other knowledge, as well.

Here are some Melodies in which Sequences may be introduced:

The following are to be harmonized according to the taste and judgment of the student. Think them out carefully and *make* them sound well.

FURTHER USES OF THE DOMINANT SEVENTH CHORD — SEQUENCES

QUESTIONS

1. How may the Dominant Seventh Chord be used, with its Fifth omitted?

2. How is the Progression of the Dominant Seventh Chord to the Submediant Chord made?

3. What is the particular use of this Progression?

4. What is a Sequence?

CHAPTER XXX
ON MELODY MAKING

The Elements of Music are **Melody**, **Rhythm** and **Harmony**.

Melody is a succession of musical sounds, arranged according to a certain order or design.

Rhythm is movement in musical time.

The student who has mastered the contents of this book up to this point knows very well what **Harmony** is.

Musical Composition is the art of building up musical ideas into larger and continuous forms.

In the Art of Music, as in all the Fine Arts, creative work is governed by certain Principles: the **Principles of Unity, Variety and Proportion.** These Principles apply just as much in the making of the simplest Melody as they do in the largest musical effort.

By **Unity** we mean oneness, individuality.

By **Variety** we mean diversity, state of difference.

By **Proportion** we mean the symmetrical relation of one part to another.

We must not observe any one of these Principles to the exclusion of the others, but we must follow each in equal measure.

The ambitious student who has reached this point should feel inspired to original creative effort. Hence, the foregoing definitions and remarks.

By the practice of Melody Making the student will acquire the ability to put his own tone thoughts into definite form and to improve his understanding of all that he may hear.

Referring to the Principles of Unity, Variety and Proportion one may find illustrations in many familiar objects. Take a piece of wall paper, for instance. There is always a Principal *Unit* which pervades the entire design. That is **Unity**. There are Lesser *Units* which serve to *vary* or to afford contrast to the Principal Unit. That is **Variety**. The Principal Unit and the Lesser Units are repeated over and over again in a symmetrical design. That is **Proportion**. Read a verse of poetry and seek similar illustrations in it. Look at a perfect piece of Architecture and find still greater illustrations. Let the student work out other illustrations.

Now for some Musical applications of our Principles. An examination of familiar melodies discloses the fact that, with but few exceptions, all seem to proceed by rhythmic groups of two or four measures, and multiples of the same.

Here are some examples:

"HOME, SWEET HOME"

"OLD FOLKS AT HOME"

ON MELODY MAKING

Let the student select two familiar Melodies, proceeding in a similar manner; write them in the space following; and indicate the portions of two and four measures as in the foregoing examples.

All good melodies are made up of similar groups, which display a relationship to one another, according to the Principles of Unity, Variety and Proportion. One finds similar relationships in the lines of a verse of good poetry. In poetry, for instance the lines are said to *Rhyme*:

"My country 'tis of *thee*,
"Sweet land of liber*ty*."

Note the *Rhyming* (similarity of sound) at the ends of the lines: *thee* and *-ty*. There is a similar *Rhyming* in these musical groups; but it may occur both at the beginning and at the end of each group.

The musical terms which are to follow are frequently employed in a very elastic manner; but, for our present purposes, we will restrict them to certain definite proportions.

The *shortest* form of Melody is *eight measures* in length. This is called a **Period**. The *Half-Period* (*four measures*) is called a **Phrase**. The *Half-Phrase* (*two measures*) is called a **Section**. The *Half-Section* (*one measure*) is called a **Motive**.

We are now going to take a *Motive* and expand it into a *Section;* the *Section* into a *Phrase;* and the *Phrase* into a *Period*. Let us take as our material, in the first place, the Major Scale, or any portion of it. This will give us a **Diatonic Melody**. **Diatonic** means proceeding by *Degrees*. We will select a simple double time ($\frac{2}{4}$) and begin on the Tonic of C Major, thus:  . Variety would suggest, going on, that we take next the Degree above C: D; and thus complete our first *Motive*: . Unity is preserved by using notes of equal value. Proportion would suggest that we complete our first *Section* by a repetition of our first *Motive*, thus: . By continuing this *Section* and repeating it in a higher Degree, we make a *Phrase* thus:

. Since we have been rising continually from our Tonic, Proportion would suggest that we now begin to fall. Let us reverse our first *Section* and carry it downward towards our Tonic: [musical notation]. Continuing this process in the next *Section*, we reach our Tonic, complete the second *Phrase*, and also complete the *Period*: [musical notation]. Here it is:

[musical notation labeled Motive, Section, Phrase, Period]

All this may seem very simple indeed, but it is necessary, in order to show how Melody is made to grow, and to aid in developing logical habits of musical thought.

Now, let the student go to work. Here is a Phrase. Let the student complete the Period, by adding a second Phrase, according to the method outlined.

[musical notation in 3/4]

Here is another one, starting downward from the Tonic.

[musical notation in 4/4]

Now let us gain more Variety by changes in Rhythm or by an additional Motive.

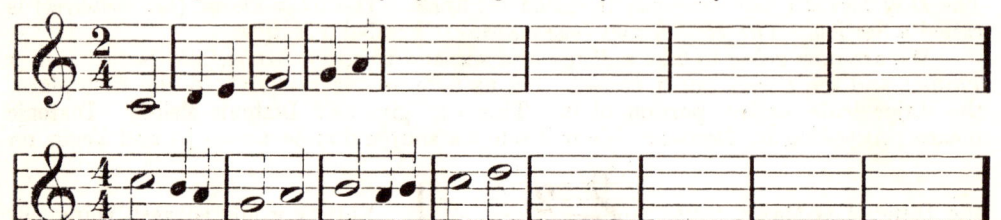

[musical notation in 2/4]

[musical notation in 4/4]

Let the student make a Diatonic Period of his own; in ¾ Time, Scale of G.

[musical notation in 3/4]

Many good Melodies are to be found which are chiefly Diatonic, with very few skips. Many are as simple in Rhythm as our present examples. Take the familiar "OLD HUNDRED", for instance. Find this tune. Play and sing it.

Diatonic Melodies are the best practice at the outset, but of course, skips may be introduced. Melodies may be constructed by deriving the Motives from Triads or Common Chords. This is also good practice. Here is a Period constructed in this manner:

[musical notation with numbered measures 1-8]

ON MELODY MAKING

Let us analyze this. Measure 1, the Principal Motive contains the Root and Third of the Tonic Chord (F, A, C). Measure 2, the Second Motive contains the Fifth (G) and the Root (C) of the Dominant Chord. Measures 3 and 4, the Second Section, are in Rhyme with Measures 1 and 2. Measure 5 starts the Second Phrase with a return to the Principle Motive. Measure 6 suggests the Subdominant Chord (B♭, D, F). Measure 7 contains the Third of the Tonic Chord (A), and the Seventh (B♭) and the Fifth (G) of the Dominant Seventh Chord. Measure 8 brings us to a close on the Tonic.

Now, let the student try some Melodies, using Diatonic Motives, occasional skips, or Motives derived from Chords. The opening Phrases, Sections or Motives are given.

Begin on some Member of the Tonic Chord, and end on the Tonic Degree.

A Minor:

G Minor:

The foregoing exercises will have served to give the student some insight into the mechanical process of melody making. It is in reality melody building. One hears much of inspiration, and doubtless many fine melodies have come through inspiration; but only after logical habits of thought have been acquired through earnest study and practice. A whole book might be written on melody making but in this Chapter we have contented ourselves with starting the student on his way. To recapitulate: follow the three artistic Principles; use only one or two Motives in any one Melody and work them out logically; let each leading Motive, Section and Phrase appear to ask a question, which the following Motive, Section, and Phrase, respectively, answers, the Period being the completed musical sentence.

Now let the student make some Periods, inventing his own Motives. We will indicate only the Scale, and the Time Signature of each one.

A Minor:

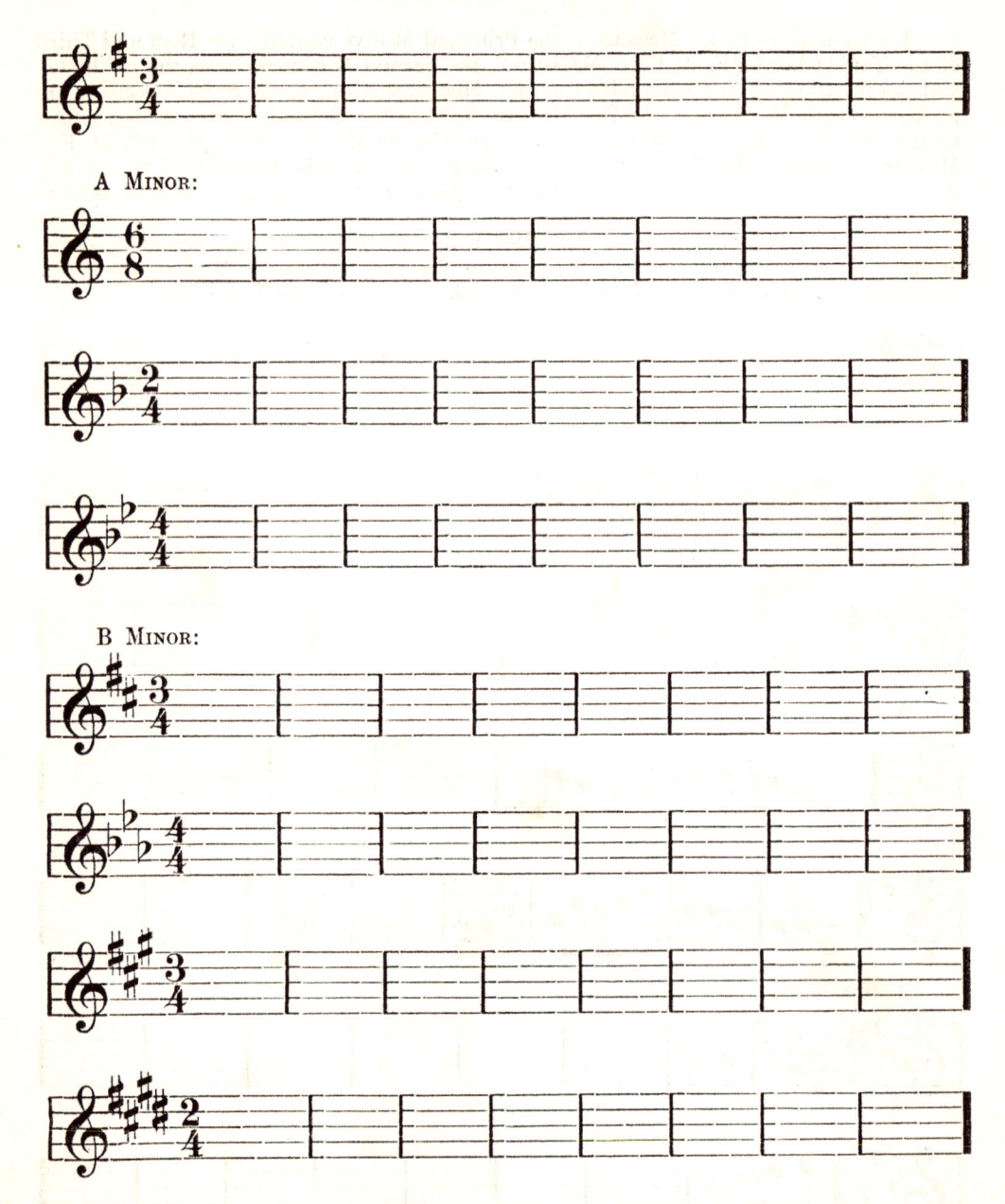

B Minor:

The student, who, after having made these Melodies, feels impelled to harmonize one or more of them according to present knowledge, will have made his first real attempt at Musical Composition.

QUESTIONS

1. What are the Elements of Music? Define each.
2. What is Musical Composition?
3. What are the three artistic Principles? Define each.
4. What is a Motive?
5. What is a Section?
6. What is a Phrase?
7. What is a Period?

The Practical Theoretical Text Books of
Preston Ware Orem

MUS. DOC.

Teacher, theorist, organist, for many years music editor of Theodore Presser Co., Dr. Orem's works reflect his practical experience in a presentation that while thorough, is lucid, easily comprehended and always intensely interesting. Specially arranged for use in classes, these works also can be of much assistance to the self-help student.

HARMONY BOOK FOR BEGINNERS

A Text Book and Writing Book for the First Year's Work—for Class, Private and Self Instruction

The main essentials of harmony are made understandable in a clear, concise manner and everything is presented simply, yet in an engaging and interesting manner. Here is a harmony book with NO RULES. Printed staves are provided, right in the book, for writing out all exercises. This gives the student a complete record of work accomplished for future use as reference. Progressing from the beginning to the dominant seventh chord the work lays a strong foundation for future musicianship. A chapter on melody-writing is included.

Flush Cloth Bound
Price, $1.25

THEORY AND COMPOSITION OF MUSIC

A Manual of Advanced Harmony, Melody Writing, Practical Composition and Musical Form

This book, designed to follow the author's **Harmony Book for Beginners,** in addition to completing the study of harmony, develops, side by side, a knowledge of melody writing, composition and musical form. The work is carried on in the same pleasing manner that has made the beginning book such an outstanding favorite. Ambitious students will eagerly grasp the opportunity afforded for a practical application of their knowledge of harmony to the art of composing.

Flush Cloth Bound
Price, $1.25

THE ART OF INTERWEAVING MELODIES

A First Method of Counterpoint for Students of All Ages

Contemporary music, as heard over the radio and in concert, reveals the composers and arrangers as thorough masters of the art of counterpoint. The study of this subject is usually regarded as rather tedious, but in **The Art of Interweaving Melodies** Dr. Orem's entertaining and lucid style makes it most fascinating. A practical, working knowledge of harmony is all the student needs to take up this work. As in his previous works the author eschews formal RULES with their vexatious EXCEPTIONS and provides a "quiz" at the close of each lesson.

Flush Cloth Bound
Price, $1.25

MANUAL OF MODULATION

◆

A Little Book of Much Value to the Organist, Student, Accompanist and the Aspiring Composer

Even accomplished performers sometimes have great difficulty in working out modulations at the keyboard. With many pianists and organists, especially those who accompany singers and instrumentalists, the ability to pass quickly from one key to another would be a great convenience. Here, in this booklet, Dr. Orem tells in a clear and understandable manner the basic principles of modulation without hanging any theoretical cobwebs before the reader's eyes.

Price, 40 cents

THEODORE PRESSER CO. MUSIC PUBLISHERS 1712 CHESTNUT ST. **PHILA., PA.**